THE EASY GUIDE TO YOUR ATARI 600XL/800XL

THE EASY GUIDE TO YOUR ATARI® 600XL™/800XL™

Thomas Blackadar

BERKELEY • PARIS • DÜSSELDORF

Cover art by Daniel Le Noury
Book design by Mary Rose Ogren

Library of Congress Card Number: 84-50365
ISBN 0-89588-125-X
Printed in the United States of America
10 9 8 7 6 5 4 3 2 1

ACKNOWLEDGEMENTS

A book such as this is always a joint project, and many people share the credit. I'd particularly like to thank Rudolph Langer and Paul Panish for their support and advice in the development of this project. Joel Kreisman contributed valuable technical assistance at all stages, and David Kolodney gave it a careful and sensitive editing. My thanks also to these other wonderful people who did so much to turn a manuscript into a book: Valerie Robbins and Leslie Horston, word processing; Gloria Maya, Valerie Brewster, and Cheryl Vega, typesetting; Janis Lund and Elizabeth Thomas, proofreading; and Mary Rose Ogren, design. Their contributions are much appreciated.

At Atari, Margaret Lasecke and her staff were extremely helpful. From my initial contacts with Bruce Quill to my final houndings of Trish Marino, everyone was friendly and cooperative.

TABLE OF CONTENTS

Appendices

INTRODUCTION

If you have recently bought an Atari® computer, you may have been surprised when you opened the box. The machine was there all right, but what about the instruction book? All you could find was a thin *Owner's Guide* and an *Atari BASIC Reference Guide,* forbiddingly marked "for experienced programmers only."

I'm sorry to have to say it, but that's all there is. Atari freely admits that it does not try to teach more than the essentials of setting up the machines. "If you want more information," they say, "you should buy a book."

Your Atari computer is a wonderful machine: it works well and can grow with your needs. I have written this book to be your guide, to help you learn quickly what you need to know about your computer.

In the course of this book, you will set up your computer and begin to use it. You will find out where you can buy programs that will let you start using your computer right away. Then you will learn how to write your own programs, and how to store them on a program recorder or disk drive.

What do you need to know beforehand? Nothing. This is an *easy guide,* which assumes you have never used a computer before. You can start from the very beginning, and move slowly enough to master the concepts without needing to cope with computer jargon.

If you know a little already, you can still use this book. You may want to skim through sections that you already understand, then read more carefully once you get to the sections you still need to cover.

I have tried to make this book both serious and enjoyable. I have assumed that you are truly interested in learning about your Atari computer, and that you want a clear, no-nonsense introduction. At the same time, I have concentrated on the most attractive, entertaining features of your Atari.

The chapters are grouped into three sections. This will help you organize your explorations into three fundamental phases: Getting Acquainted, Programming, and Storage.

The first section, Getting Acquainted, will help you learn the fundamentals of your machine. Before you can do anything else, you must learn how the computer works and how to type simple commands. By playing around with the machine, you will become comfortable using it.

Section Two moves into programming. You can combine simple commands into a larger plan in order to perform more complex tasks. As you learn the concepts of computer programming, you will also be learning BASIC, the primary language used by Atari computers and one of the computer languages most commonly used today.

Section Three addresses a subject treated only briefly earlier: how to store your programs permanently on tapes or diskettes. Chapter 9 describes how to use the Atari Program Recorder with cassette tapes. Chapter 10 shows how to use a disk drive for faster, more reliable storage. At some points in this book, you may want to glance ahead to these chapters, if you want to use commercial programs or store your own programs for future reference.

To use this book most effectively, you will need to have access to an Atari computer. For most of the book, you should have your computer sitting in front of you, so that you can try out the examples as you read.

It doesn't matter which Atari computer you have. This book is directed specifically at the new Atari 600XL™ and 800XL™, but the descriptions will also work for the other Atari models. The projected Atari 1400XL™ and 1450XLD™ will both be essentially the same machine as the 800XL, with some additional features. Everything said in this book will also apply to them, and any differences will be noted in the text.

If you have one of the older Ataris (the discontinued 400™, 800™, and 1200XL™ models), you will need Atari's *BASIC Computing Language* cartridge to use this book. If you plug this cartridge in, your computer will behave just like an Atari 600XL or 800XL, and you can run any program just as if you had one of the new machines. There may, however, be a few differences in the details about the keyboard and graphics. Read pages 6–8 of Chapter 1 if you are thinking of using this book with a model other than the 600XL or 800XL.

Computers may seem mysterious while you are an outsider, but after your first steps, you will be able to continue on your own. This book merely aims to make those first steps a little easier.

Section 1

Getting Acquainted

CHAPTER ONE

Meet the Atari Computers

You have recently bought an Atari computer, and are anxious to start using it. You are curious to find out what your machine can do, and how you can control it.

This chapter is an overview. It gives some tips that will help you become comfortable with your Atari, and detailed instructions on how to set it up. By the end of the chapter, you will be ready to use your computer.

FEAR

Before you begin your journey, you'll need to overcome your fears. If this is your first time on a computer, you are probably a little intimidated by it. You don't have to be: a computer is a machine, nothing more. Like a television set or a dishwasher, a computer can help you if you learn how to use it, and it won't bite you if you make a mistake.

You don't need to be afraid that you might wreck your computer by pressing the wrong key. Your computer is an electronic device that deserves the same care you give to a radio or a pocket calculator, but you don't have to be timid with it. There is little you can do in normal use that will harm it. At the very worst, you might lose the words and numbers you have just typed, but you won't hurt the machine.

Your Atari gives you a kind of panic button. This is the RESET key, located along the right side of the keyboard. If you ever get lost or don't know what's happening, you can always press this key. The computer will go back to the way it was when you turned it on, ready to start again. And if that doesn't do the trick, you can always turn the power off and back on.

If you have some lingering fears, play a game. There is no better way to become comfortable with a computer than to have fun with it. In Chapter 2 of this book, you will find out how to buy some of the best Atari games, but for now, you might want to start with the most famous: Pac-Man. Atari's home version of this game is truly excellent—a sure-fire cure for computer fear.

WHAT IS A COMPUTER?

How does a computer work? You don't need to know. You can think of it as a closed box that takes in information, churns it around, and spits out the results. Along the way, it must do many complex operations, but that's not something you need to concern yourself with. Just think about what goes in and what comes out.

You talk to the computer through its *keyboard.* Atari computers have a full set of typewriter keys that let you type letters, numbers, and special symbols. You will use these keys for all your contact with the computer.

To talk back, the computer has an electronic circuit that can display words and pictures on your television screen. So, as you type letters on the keyboard, your computer shows them on the screen. Then, if it needs to give an answer, it displays that as well. With *graphics,* you can also have the computer draw pictures on the screen.

The computer has a *memory,* so that you can store information for future reference. You can use this memory to save the lines of a program, the numbers you will use in a future calculation, or the words of a text you are writing.

How much you can store at any one time depends on the size of your computer's memory, which is measured in *bytes.* A byte is roughly the space needed to store a single letter or a three-digit number. You will often see memory listed with letter K, which means roughly a thousand bytes (1024 to be exact). One K would hold about one third of this page.

For the purposes of this book, you won't need to worry about the size of your computer's memory. The Atari 600XL has 16K bytes of memory built in—more than enough for anything in this book. The other Ataris have even more. Later on, you may want to buy a memory expansion for the 600XL so that you can run more complicated programs.

One other thing about your computer's memory: everything you store in it is erased when you turn the power off. To store information permanently, you must attach a *program recorder* or a *disk drive.*

WHAT CAN IT DO?

Your Atari computer can perform complex calculations quickly and easily, display bar graphs, and paint colorful pictures on your television screen. With a word-processing program, it can let you revise a letter without retyping it. And of course, it can play games.

The computer's great strength is its flexibility. It can do numerical calculations if you wish, or limit itself to letters and words. It can react to the keyboard and arrange the screen display in any way you wish. With its memory, it can store and arrange information in a variety of useful ways.

You control your computer with a *program,* a detailed list of instructions that it follows like a recipe, step-by-step, to perform its task. The program can be as simple or as complicated as you like, and can ask the computer to make decisions as it works. Programs are often called *software.*

A good way to start is to buy programs that other people have written. When you use commercial software, you don't need to know how it works. You just give general instructions and answer a few questions, then let the program take care of the details. Chapter 2 of this book is an introduction to some of the software that is commercially available. Games are very popular, and the Atari computers have by far the best selection of entertainment software of any home computer. You can, however, also buy programs for many other purposes, such as education and home management. Word processing has become increasingly popular among those who want the convenience of an electronic typewriter.

At some point, however, you may want to write your own programs, to gain direct control over your computer. Commercial programs are expensive and sometimes inconvenient. If you plan to use your computer to its full potential, you will want direct control. In the later chapters of this book, you will learn how to write your own programs. This will let you tell your computer exactly what you want it to do. At the same time, it will let you explore many of the computer's deeper capabilities, so that you will be the master of your machine.

THE ATARI COMPUTERS

Atari has sold many different computers since it entered the business. To avoid confusion, I'd like to explain their history and their minor differences. Figure 1.1 is a comparison chart of the models. They can be divided into two groups: new and old.

The new ones, sold starting late in 1983, all contain XL in their model numbers and feature a sharp-looking white-and-brown case. Of these new machines, two were available as this book was going to press: the low-priced 600XL and 800XL. Two others, the 1400XL and 1450XLD, were still under development. Rumor has it that one or even both of these may be cancelled, or never even introduced. They are mentioned in this book for the sake of completeness, but are not covered in detail.

Before Atari introduced these new machines, it had been selling two

FEATURES	600XL (available)	800XL	1400XL (planned)	1450XLD	400 (discontinued)	800	1200XL
Memory size	16K	64K	64K	64K	16K	48K	64K
Typewriter-style keyboard	•	•	•	•	*	•	•
XL-style design	•	•	•	•			•
Programmable function keys			•	•			•
Built-in BASIC	•	•	•	•			
Monitor connection		•	•	•		•	•
Telephone connection			•	•			
Speech synthesizer			•	•			
Built-in disk drive				•			
Graphics modes	11	11	11	11	6–9	6–9	11
Text modes	5	5	5	5	3	3	5

**flat keyboard*

Figure 1.1: *The features of the Atari computers.*

others: the Atari 400 and the 800. In between, there was the Atari 1200XL, an intermediate model that was sold for only a few months.

Fortunately, all of these models are just variations on the same machine. The older models lack a few features, and require that you plug in a separate BASIC language cartridge. Some of the new XL computers have extras built in, but for the most part the machines are functionally identical, and all run the same programs.

This book is directed primarily at the Atari 600XL, shown in Figure 1.2, and at the 800XL, a larger version with more memory. However, you can also use this book with any of Atari's other computers, old or new. All of the programs described here will work on the new machines, and the physical descriptions should vary only in minor details. If you own one of the older computers (400, 800, or 1200XL), you will need to make only a few small allowances.

Why all these different models? Atari has tried to design a line of computers that will appeal to everyone. It sells the Atari 600XL for those who want merely the basic machine for games and simple programming. For those who want a more powerful machine, it sells two higher-priced models, each of which adds features to the one before. The machines are so similar, however, that you can make the 600XL into any of the others merely by adding external devices.

If you add a memory-expansion module to an Atari 600XL, it effectively becomes an 800XL. The future 1400XL and 1450XLD will be the same as the 600XL and 800XL, but with some extra

Figure 1.2: This book is aimed at the Atari 600XL. The 800XL is essentially the same, but with additional memory.

features. They will contain a *telephone modem,* which will allow them to transmit programs and information to other computers over the telephone. They will also include a *speech synthesizer,* which lets the computer pronounce English words out loud. The 1450XLD will have, in addition, a built-in disk drive and a space for a second one. If you buy one of these machines, you can initially learn to use it just as if it were a 600XL, and then move on to master its additional features.

If you have one of the Atari 400, 800, or 1200XL models that were sold before the end of 1983, you can still use this book, but you will have to be more careful. To begin with, the physical design of the machine is different from the new models, and some of the keys have been changed. As you read about the keyboard in Chapter 3, you will need to adjust some of the details to fit your machine.

Another difference involves graphics. While the basic graphic-display systems are the same in both the old and new Ataris, the XL versions have several additional graphics modes. Some of these are discussed in Chapter 8. If you have one of the older machines, you will not be able to use these advanced graphics features, but you will have no problems with the rest of this book.

Unlike the new models, the discontinued Atari 400, 800, and 1200XL do not have the BASIC programming language built in. If you want to do anything more than run commercial software, you will have to buy Atari's BASIC Computing Language cartridge. *To use this book with one of the older computers, you must have this BASIC cartridge plugged in.* Figure 1.3 lists the Atari computers and describes what allowances, if any, you will need to make as you read on.

SETTING UP YOUR COMPUTER

The only thing you'll need that does not come with your computer is a television set. You can use any normal television, but you will get the best results from newer models. Televisions more than ten years old may give a jittery screen image.

A color television is strongly recommended. The Atari computers have a spectacular color graphics system that can display 256 different shades. Many of the programs in this book take advantage of these displays. While you can run them on a black-and-white television, you will be missing a lot.

If you are selecting a television to use with your computer, you

Atari 600XL	This book was written specifically for this machine. No special adjustments are necessary.
Atari 800XL	This machine is essentially an Atari 600XL with extra memory. You can use this book as if you had a 600XL.
Atari 1400XL (projected)	If it becomes available, this machine will be the same as the Atari 800XL, except that it will have a larger keyboard and some added features. You can use this book, but it will not describe the built-in telephone modem or the speech synthesizer.
Atari 1450XLD (projected)	Like the 1400XL, this model is still in the planning stage. When it appears, it will have all of the same features as the 1400XL, plus a disk drive. For the basic computer, however, you can still use this book.
Atari 400 (discontinued)	This older machine has the same internal operation as the Atari 600XL. Its flat keyboard makes it harder to use than the other Atari computers. The physical descriptions in Chapter 3, and the advanced graphics in Chapter 8 will be somewhat different. YOU MUST HAVE AN ATARI BASIC CARTRIDGE.
Atari 800 (discontinued)	This older machine has the same internal operation as the Atari 800XL. The physical descriptions in Chapter 3, and the advanced graphics in Chapter 8 will be somewhat different. YOU MUST HAVE AN ATARI BASIC CARTRIDGE.
Atari 1200XL (discontinued)	This discontinued machine looks the same as the Atari 1400XL, but does not have the telephone modem, speech synthesizer, or built-in BASIC. To use it, YOU MUST HAVE AN ATARI BASIC CARTRIDGE. In all other respects, it resembles the machines described in this book.

Figure 1.3: *How to use this book with any Atari computer.*

should probably choose a small or medium-size screen. Screens measuring from 10 to 15 inches are quite large enough to be readable. Larger screens are unnecessary, and often harder to read.

All the Ataris except the 600XL and the discontinued 400 allow you to hook up a *color monitor* instead of a television. A monitor looks like a television, but lacks a tuner and thus cannot be used to receive normal broadcasts. A monitor will usually give a clearer picture than a normal television. Some monitors also give you higher *resolution* (finer detail), so that with some additional equipment you can display more than 40 characters per line.

When you open the box, you will find an owner's manual and several pieces of equipment. Unpack the box carefully, and make sure you don't lose anything. You should find three major items.

First, there is the computer itself. Set this on the table where you will be working and turn it around so that you can see the back, as shown in Figure 1.4. Models other than the 600XL will look slightly different.

The second item in the box is a *power supply*, which converts your house's electricity into the direct current used by your computer. This box has a power cord and a cable that you plug into the back of the computer.

The last items you will find are a short cable and a small *switch box* that you will use to connect the computer to your television. The cable and switch box come in several forms, but the most common is shown in Figure 1.5. The box has a small black pin that you can slide between two positions. When it is in the COMPUTER position, your

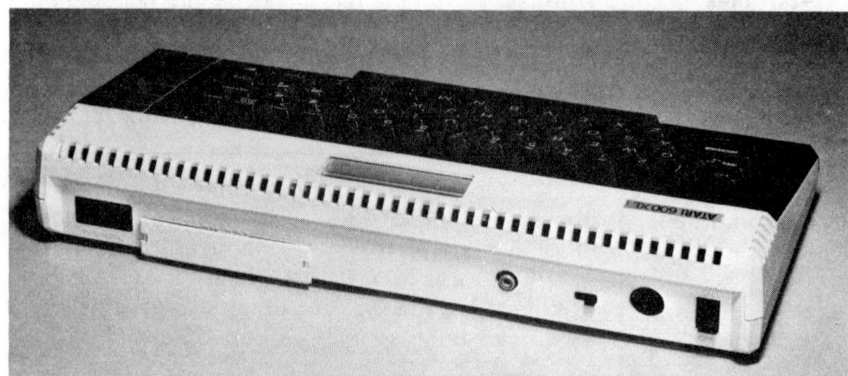

Figure 1.4: *The back of the Atari 600XL, where you will make your connections.*

television will display the computer's images. Slide the pin back into the TV position to watch normal programs.

Once you've checked that you have everything, you can connect your computer. You can easily do this yourself with nothing more than a screwdriver.

Before you start, make sure your television and computer are turned off. None of the cables is dangerous to touch, but it is a good practice always to turn the power off before making connections.

Don't be confused by the label POWER at the lower-right corner of the Atari 600XL and 800XL keyboard. This label refers to the red indicator light that shows when the power is on. The actual on/off switch is located on the back of the computer, at the left end. On the 1200XL, 1400XL, and 1450XLD, it is along the left side of the computer, next to the cartridge slot. On the 400 and 800, the switch is on the right side of the machine. The switch is always marked POWER or PWR ON/OFF.

Start by connecting the switch box to your television. Disconnect

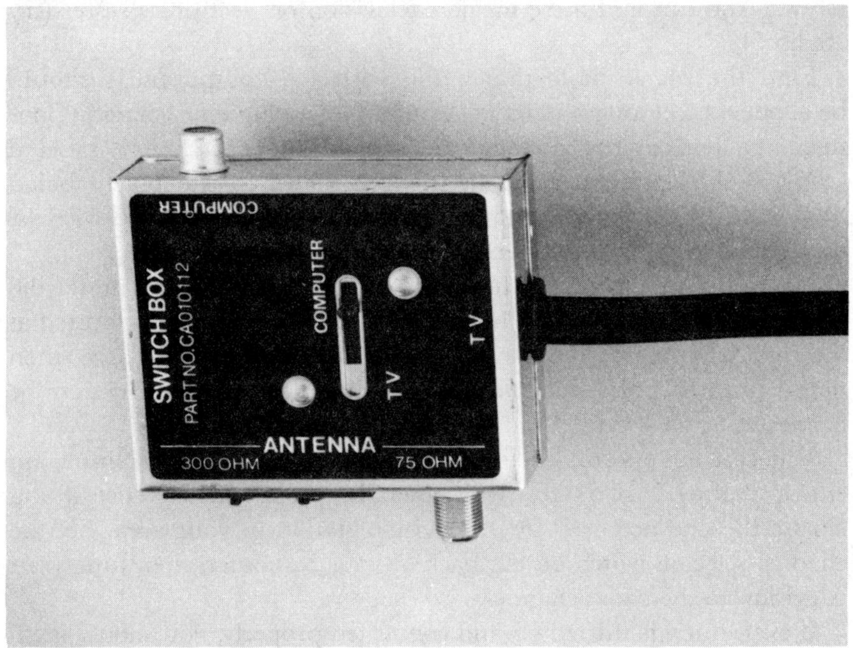

Figure 1.5: *The switch box.*

the antenna or rabbit ears. On most sets, the antenna is connected with a double cable to two screws on the back of the set labeled VHF. Loosen these screws and remove the wires. You don't need to disconnect the antenna labeled UHF. (If you are connected to a cable TV system, see below.)

The switch box has a pair of short wires coming out of one end. Connect these wires to the two screws from which you just disconnected the antenna. Tighten the screws.

On the side of the switch box labeled TV or ANTENNA, you will find another pair of screws. If you plan to use your set for normal television as well as for your computer display, attach the wires from your antenna to these screws. When the switch is set to the TV position, your antenna will be connected through the switch box just as if you had never removed it from the set.

If you subscribe to a cable network, your television is probably connected with a single round plug instead of a pair of screws. Some Atari switchboxes do have a large round connector next to the two screws; you can use this if it fits the plug on the end of your cable. If it does not fit, you will have to buy an adapter that connects to the screws. You can find these in most television or electronics stores (try Radio Shack).

Find the black cable that came with the computer. It should be about six feet long and have a round metal plug on each end. Connect one end to the hole in the side of the switch box labeled COMPUTER. Then connect the other end to the hole labeled SWITCH BOX on the computer itself. On all the new XL models, this hole is to the right of center as you face the back.

Now plug in the power supply. On all Atari XL computers, the power supply plugs into the hole labeled PWR.IN, which is located at the right as you face the back. Connect the power supply here, then plug it into an outlet in your house. Your computer should now be connected as in Figure 1.6.

You can have your television receive the computer's signal on either channel 2 or 3. You will generally get less interference if you choose the one not used by a television station in your area. Set the channel-selector switch on the back of your computer, then tune your television to the same channel.

If everything is turned on and connected properly, you should see a blue screen with the word READY in the upper-left corner. If the image is fuzzy, adjust the fine tuning on your television. If the screen isn't dark blue, adjust the color, tint, and brightness controls on your set. You may find you'll need to turn off the automatic fine tuning (AFT) or automatic color controls: some televisions provide a better image when adjusted manually.

By the way, don't worry if the screen color starts changing after a few minutes. Atari computers are designed to do this if you leave them on without doing anything. This is a useful feature, designed to protect your television. If the computer did not shift the colors, its letters could become permanently burned into the screen. The computer returns to the blue screen when you type any key.

If you can't get a picture or the image will not become clear, you may have done something wrong. The problem could be any of the following:

- You have forgotten to turn the computer or the television on, or have forgotten to plug them in.
- The cable from the computer to the switch box is not connected securely. Try wiggling the connections.
- You have not tightened the wires from the switch box securely to the VHF screws on the television.
- The switch box is not in the COMPUTER position.
- Your television is not tuned to the same channel (2 or 3) as your computer. Try changing to the other channel.

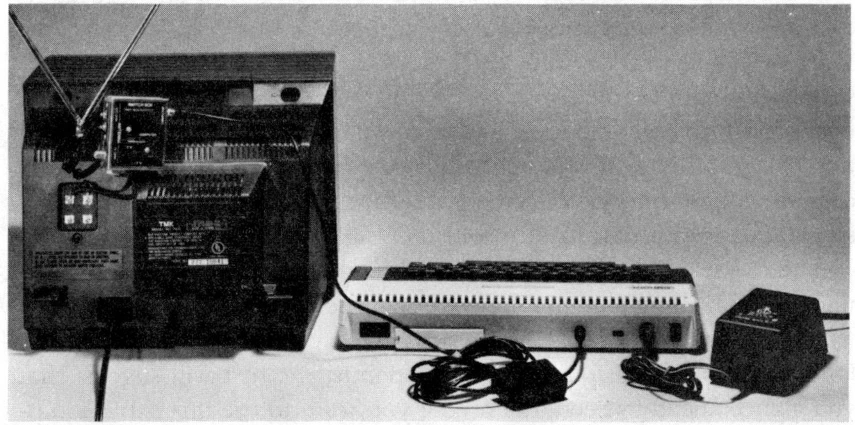

Figure 1.6: *Connecting the computer to the television.*

If you have checked all of these and your computer still doesn't work, you should contact your dealer. The machine you have bought could be defective, or you might be missing something. Your Atari dealer can give you advice, and can replace defective equipment. If you can't get satisfactory service from your dealer, call Atari's customer service hotline (800-538-8543; in California 800-672-1404).

PERIPHERAL EQUIPMENT

With a television set and the equipment that came with your computer, you have everything you'll need to use this book. You can run your computer, write BASIC programs, and use cartridge programs sold by other companies.

There are, however, a variety of devices you can attach to your computer to expand its capabilities. None of these *peripherals* is essential, but some will make your life easier.

If you are planning to play games, you will probably want to buy a *joystick.* It has a handle that you can move in various directions to control figures on the screen. It also has a small red *fire button,* used in some video games to fire shots. Your Atari lets you connect a second joystick for games in which two people play at the same time.

You may want to use the Atari Program Recorder with your computer. This device lets you *save* programs and data permanently on a standard cassette tape, so that they are not lost when the computer is turned off. Later on, you can *load* them back into the computer for reuse. The program recorder also lets you use games and programs that are sold as prerecorded cassettes.

Cassette tapes, unfortunately, tend to be slow and cumbersome. If you are doing a lot of serious work, you might want to buy a *disk drive* instead, which lets you store and retrieve large quantities of information very rapidly. A program that takes several minutes to load from a cassette might require only a few seconds with a disk drive. Also, some advanced programs are sold only for a disk drive.

The cassette recorder and disk drive are described in this book, but not until Chapters 9 and 10. There may be times earlier in the book when you will want to use these devices if you have them—to save a long program, for instance. At these points, the text will suggest that you glance ahead to Section Three if you want to use this extra equipment. In this way, you can learn to use the cassette recorder or disk drive if you have one, but you will not be distracted if you don't.

You may also want to add a *printer* to your system. As its name suggests, this lets your computer print numbers and letters on paper. This is especially useful if you want a paper copy of programs you are writing, or if you want to do word processing.

Atari makes several printers of different kinds and qualities. The cheapest is the 1020 printer/plotter, which displays text and graphics on a 4-inch-wide tape. For a little more money, you can buy a printer that uses full-size sheets of typing paper. One of these, the 1025 *dot-matrix printer,* displays letters as an array of small points. While it prints quickly and legibly, the output is not terribly attractive. For higher quality, you should consider the new 1027 *letter-quality printer,* which prints characters that resemble a normal typewriter's.

The program recorder, disk drive, and printer all connect to the same large hole in the back of the computer, labeled PERIPHERAL. If you want to use more than one device at a time, you can *chain* them together. Connect a cable between the PERIPHERAL hole on the computer and one of the holes in the back of the first device. Then connect a cable between the second device and the hole you didn't use on the first. In this way, you can have several different peripherals connected to your computer. You can connect the devices in any sequence, except for the program recorder, which must come at the end of the chain.

One other note about Atari's line of peripherals: When Atari introduced its new XL computers, it also redesigned its entire line of peripherals. Fortunately, the company has taken great care to make sure that all of its old and new machines are compatible. All of the old peripherals will work on the new machines, and all of the new peripherals will work on the old line. Figure 1.7 shows how the model

DEVICE:	OLD MODEL	NEW MODEL
Program Recorder	410	1010
Disk Drive	810	1050
Printer (4" tape)	820	1020
Printer (dot matrix)	825	1025
Printer (letter quality)	—	1027

Figure 1.7: *The old and new Atari peripherals.*

numbers correspond. Check with your dealer if you have any doubts about compatibility.

We have now reached the end of the preliminaries. You have set up your machine, and it is waiting to go. With the next chapter, you will start using it. Good luck, and enjoy yourself.

CHAPTER TWO

Commercial Software

In the first chapter, you found out what your Atari computer is, and what the features of your model are. You found out something about how the computer works, and learned that you don't need to be afraid of it. Finally, you have set it up and turned it on. Your screen says READY, and you are eager to do something.

The best way to begin using your computer is to buy programs written by other people. In many cases, you can simply plug the program into the computer and start it running. You don't need to know anything about how the computer works, and you need no programming knowledge.

You can buy all sorts of software from Atari and other manufacturers. Games are the most popular, but excellent programs are also available in other areas, such as education, home finance, and music.

This chapter will start by describing the range of what is available. While this is not a full buyer's guide, it will give you some tips on good programs. It will also discuss some of the things you should know as you shop, so that you can protect yourself from the bad programs that are sold alongside the good.

The second part of this chapter will show you how to use programs you have bought. Most programs come with instruction books that explain the details of operation, but I can give you some general guidance to help get you going.

HOW TO BUY SOFTWARE

Atari itself sells more than 250 programs for its own computers, and claims that more than 2,000 are available from other sources.

From this large selection, you should have no trouble finding some that suit your needs.

Programs are sold for the Atari computers on cartridges, cassettes, or disks. Games tend to be sold as cartridges, while more serious programs are usually sold on tape or disk.

A cartridge stores its program in an electronic circuit, which the computer can read directly. Because they plug directly into the computer and cannot be erased, cartridges are generally more convenient and more durable than other forms of software.

Prerecorded cassettes are used with the Atari Program Recorder. With cassettes, the program is encoded as variations in a high-pitched whistle. The computer can decode, store, and use these messages. Cassette tapes have several important drawbacks. Before you can use them, you have to load the program into the computer's memory. This loading procedure can be a little complicated, even if you follow the procedure in Chapter 9 of this book. Cassettes are slow, taking as long as five minutes to load a complex program. They are also less durable than cartridges, and can be made unreadable by magnetic fields or mechanical wear.

A disk drive is more convenient. This device uses 5¼-inch plates called *diskettes* covered with a magnetic recording surface that can store large amounts of information. You still have to load diskette programs into the computer before you use them, but the procedure is faster and more reliable than with cassette tapes. Most software manufacturers sell their cassette programs in diskette form as well. Diskettes and disk drives are described in Chapter 10.

You can buy programs for your Atari computer at most places that sell Atari computers or video-game machines. Department and discount stores usually carry some programs, especially the more popular games. Many record and television stores now also carry software for home computers. In large cities, you can usually find stores that specialize in computer software. These are your best bet for finding the less popular titles.

Atari's own programs are usually very good. Atari deserves its reputation for fine video games, and it has an excellent line of home-management programs as well. While Atari does occasionally let a mediocre program slip through, it has very good overall quality. Atari also runs a service called APX (for Atari Program EXchange), which sells programs submitted by Atari users. Many of these titles are quite useful, though they tend to be unpolished. Most APX programs are sold on diskette.

A number of other companies sell programs that run on Atari computers. Atari has wisely encouraged this practice in the belief that a wide selection of software will help to sell its machines. These independent companies are called *third-party manufacturers*.

If you choose your programs off the shelf, you will learn an unpleasant fact: mixed in with the truly excellent programs, there are many poor ones. In the fast-moving computer business, some companies have been able to sell inferior products merely by wrapping them up in attractive packages. Even Atari has sometimes been guilty of rushing programs to the market before they were really ready. Since you usually have no way to look at the program before you buy it, you can easily make mistakes.

There are several resources that can help you. Addison-Wesley publishes an index of Atari programs called *The Book of Atari Software,* for $19.95. While the catalog format is a little unwieldy, this book does give short descriptions and ratings of most of the programs currently available.

Magazines are also helpful. *Compute!* is a general monthly magazine that often reviews new programs offered for Atari home computers. *ANTIC,* a magazine devoted to the Atari computers, often describes new products.

GAMES

I would suggest you start with a game if you are using your computer for the first time. You can do more serious work later.

You can buy many types of games for your Atari computer. Atari has made its name with its large selection of excellent video games, many of which became famous in the video arcades. Game programs usually cost between $25 and $40.

You will generally need to have a joystick to play games. Atari's joystick costs less than $10, and can be found at any dealer or discount store. If you are a serious game player, you might want to invest in a fancier joystick, for greater comfort and better control. For certain games, you might also consider an arcade-style *trackball,* which lets you control your players by rolling a ball in the direction you want to move. These cost between $50 and $75.

Of the arcade games available for the Atari computers, Pac-Man is the most famous. Figure 2.1 shows the home computer version of the game. Your object is to move your small yellow man around the maze and eat all of the dots, without being caught by one of the four roving monsters. You can achieve temporary safety by eating one of the larger "energizer" dots in the four corners of the screen. This allows you to chase the monsters and eat them instead of being eaten. After a short time, however, you must return to your task of eating dots and avoiding monsters.

Pac-Man is an excellent bargain. Atari's home-computer version is very well designed, and retains all of the important features of the arcade game. Even if you aren't a video-game fanatic, the Pac-Man cartridge will give you a fine introduction to some of the things your computer can do.

Atari sells several other video games for its home computers. Centipede and Missile Command are familiar titles from the video arcade. In Star Raiders, an original Atari game, you pilot a spaceship in a battle against a fleet of enemy attackers. You must plan your strategy

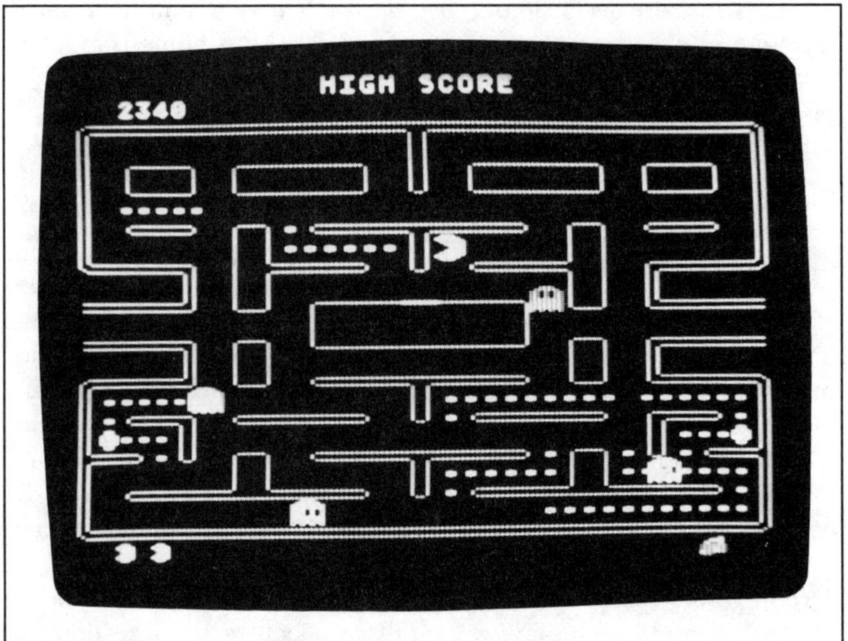

Figure 2.1: *The Pac-Man game.*

carefully to conserve your fuel and protect your defensive shields. As you fly, you see a view of the stars and your enemy's ships moving by.

Of the games made by other companies for Atari computers, my personal favorite is Serpentine, by Brøderbund Software. In this game, shown in Figure 2.2, you maneuver a small snake around a maze, trying to catch three enemy snakes from behind without letting them catch you. Brøderbund also sells the popular game Choplifter!, in which you fly a helicopter behind enemy lines trying to rescue 64 hostages.

You should remember that you can buy more than just video games. Chess is one of the most interesting games you can play against the computer. Atari's Computer Chess cartridge plays quite a respectable game, and is easy to use.

Many people enjoy *adventure games.* Unlike a video game, an adventure usually requires no fast shooting or quick action. Instead, it places you in an imaginary situation, and asks you to find a treasure or solve a problem. Two of the most popular are Zork, by Infocom, and the Scott-Adams Adventure Series, by Adventure International.

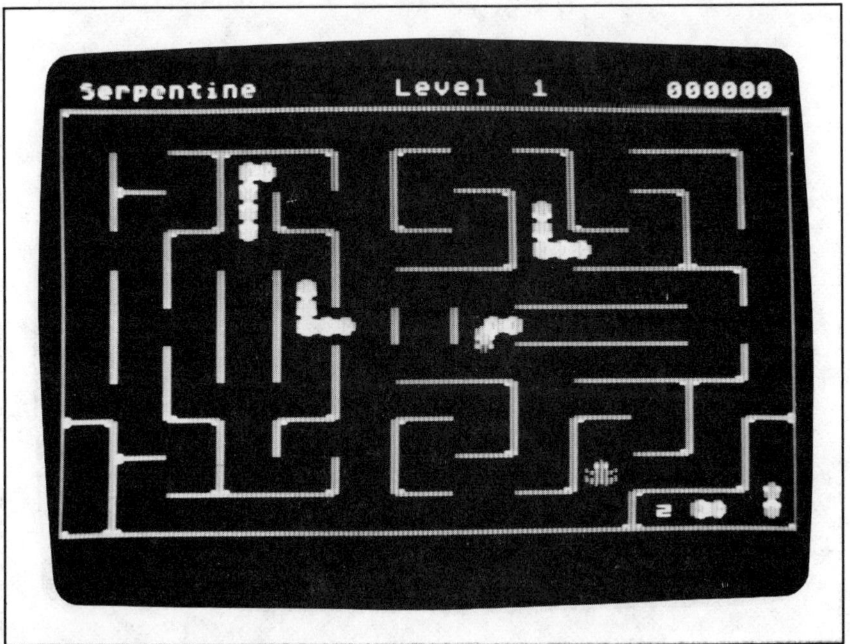

Figure 2.2: *The Serpentine game, by Brøderbund Software.*

You play an adventure by typing short commands, such as "climb stairs" or "look under the table." If it can understand you, the computer will do as you direct and then describe the results. You must often be very resourceful to find your way around an obstacle in the imaginary universe.

A final title worth mentioning is Shamus, by Synapse Software. This game, shown in Figure 2.3, combines the best elements of video and adventure games. You must explore an unknown dungeon, in search of the keys and keyholes that will let you escape. In each room, you must combat numerous monsters, shooting and dodging as you would in a video game. You get the fast action of the video arcade and the careful strategy of a dungeon adventure in a single game.

SERIOUS PROGRAMS

Atari and other companies sell many useful programs that can help you in serious work as well. Education, home finance, and word processing are only a few of the things for which you can use your computer.

Figure 2.3: *The Shamus game, by Synapse Software.*

Many people buy programs to help their children's education. A computer program can give a child individual attention and colorful, animated illustrations of concepts. It can check his work each step of the way, correcting his mistakes as he makes them. Some people also feel that a child who is exposed to a computer at an early age will be more comfortable with a machine that may play a large part in his future.

Of the educational programs available for the Atari computers, my favorites are those made by Spinnaker Software. That company's Facemaker, designed for preschoolers, is one of the most entertaining programs available, yet it is effective in teaching basic skills of memory, recognition, and creativity. With this program, your child can put a face together on the screen, choosing from a selection of hairstyles, eyebrows, noses, and mouths. He can also play a memory game that challenges him to recall a lengthening series of facial expressions. Spinnaker sells several other fine educational programs, including Kindercomp and Snooper Troops.

If you want to introduce your children to programming on the computer, you might consider Atari's PILOT. This is a simplified programming language that lets a child explore the computer by creating graphic designs on the screen. It is sold as a plug-in cartridge.

Complex financial calculations haunt many homeowners. A number of computer programs are available that can simplify such tasks as calculating loan payments, making a budget, or keeping household records. You may be amazed at how much easier it becomes to deal with your financial problems.

Unfortunately, two of Atari's best financial programs require a disk drive. The Home Filing Manager lets you keep records on electronic index cards. When you need a piece of information, you can search through your file in any way you wish. For instance, you can retrieve all of the entries that contain a certain name or telephone number. The program's attractive screen display even looks like a deck of index cards, right down to the paper clip with which you mark important entries. The Home Filing Manager would be useful for any type of organized record-keeping, such as a mailing list or a teacher's grade book. It sells for $49.95.

VisiCalc, which runs only on a disk drive and requires 32K of memory, is another resource for financial management. This famous program was the first of the electronic *spreadsheets,* which are popular in the business world. The program gives you a large, freeform table, with many rows and columns. You type numbers and labels into the cells of this table in any way you wish. You can then use the resources of your computer to add figures or perform complex calculations. This program would be useful for anyone who needs to keep track of charts of numbers. Its suggested retail price is $199.95.

The other program that might help you is the AtariWriter word processor. When you plug this cartridge in, your Atari computer acts as an intelligent typewriter. You start by typing your text into the computer's memory. You can then edit it by inserting words, deleting sentences, and moving blocks of text around. Once your text looks the way you want it, you type a command to print it. This program requires a printer and either a program recorder or disk drive.

You can buy programs to do many other things with your Atari computer. Music programs, such as the Atari Composer, let you play melodies through your computer's sound system. Atari's Paint program lets you draw colorful pictures on the screen.

HOW TO USE SOFTWARE

There's no real trick to using preprogrammed software. You just turn the computer on, give some simple commands, and let the program run. When the program needs some information from you, it will usually ask you for it with a simple message on the screen. The best programs are organized so that they actually help you organize your thinking, and give you help when you need it.

With a cartridge, you just plug the program into the computer and turn it on. On the Atari 600XL and 800XL, the cartridge plugs into the large hole in the top of the computer, which is covered by a pair of silvered doors. On the 1200XL and 1400XL, the cartridge slides into the large hole along the left side. On the discontinued Atari 400 and 800 models, you will need to open the small door on the top of the machine, then push the cartridge into one of the slots inside.

With cassettes or diskettes, you must load the program into the computer's memory before you can use it. Start by connecting the program recorder or disk drive to the computer, plugging the heavy cable into the PERIPHERAL connection in back. With a cassette, you must normally turn on the computer and type a command on the keyboard to tell it to LOAD the program. With a diskette, the computer will usually load the program automatically if you turn it on with the disk in the disk drive. Most software packages include detailed instructions on how to load the program. If you can't figure out how to do this, refer to chapters 9 and 10 of this book.

If you are using the 600XL or one of the other XL computers, you may have trouble with a few programs that were originally written for the older Atari computers (the 400 and 800). While most programs are compatible with both the old and new models, a few are not. In the cases where the programs are not compatible, the software companies have generally prepared an updated version that will work on all machines. You should contact your dealer to exchange the program.

When using some older diskette programs on an XL model, you must hold down the OPTION key as you turn on the computer. You must do this because many older programs assumed that you had removed the BASIC programming language cartridge from the computer before you loaded the program. Since BASIC is built into the new computers and cannot be removed, you must use the OPTION key to disable the language.

Once you have the program loaded, the going is easy. The better programs give you full directions right on the screen. You can usually read the instruction manual for further explanation.

A LOOK AHEAD

This chapter has shown you how to use programs written and sold by other people. In it, you have seen some of the things you can do with your Atari computer with no experience whatsoever. By using preprogrammed software, you can learn about your machine and start it working for you immediately.

You can do a lot more with your computer if you learn to give commands and write programs on your own. You will be in direct control of your machine, rather than following along the lines someone else has laid out.

The next two chapters will show you some of the basics of using your computer. You will learn how to use the keyboard and how to display words on the screen. You will learn the fundamentals of your Atari computer's graphics system, so that you can draw pictures as well.

Then, in Section Two, you will find out about real programming.

In this, you will combine the concepts you have learned in Chapters 3 and 4 into larger means of control. If you work slowly through all of the examples, you will finish this guide with a good, firm knowledge of your computer.

CHAPTER THREE

The Keyboard and the Screen

In this chapter, you will learn about your computer's keyboard. For the most part, you will use it to type words and numbers just as you would use a typewriter. However, there are several special keys that you must also master so that you can control what the computer is doing. These are all described in the following pages.

At the same time, you will also learn how to control the words your computer displays on your television screen. You will find that the screen has two functions. It works with the keyboard, repeating everything you type so that you can see what you have written, and it displays the computer's responses to your commands.

This chapter will introduce a simple command called PRINT, which lets you display a single line of text or numbers on the screen. As you learn more about this command, you will be able to position the text where you want it and to clear unwanted clutter from your screen.

Some of this may seem trivial. Why should you want to go through all this trouble just to have the computer say HELLO? Why should you care about commands that let you clear the screen? Be patient. These are building blocks for the rest of the book. Before you can do anything more complicated, you will need to know how to type commands into your computer and how to interpret its responses. Once you've passed this step, you'll be able to do many interesting things.

THE KEYBOARD

The Atari computer's keyboard is shown in Figure 3.1. It looks very much like a normal typewriter, with a few things added. The letters are all in the same places, and only a few symbols have been moved. You might notice a few unfamiliar keys at the left and right sides of the keyboard, but for the most part, you can use it like a typewriter.

Turn on your computer and your television set. If you are set up correctly, your television screen will be dark blue, with the word READY in the upper-left corner. If you can't get your screen to look like this, reread the instructions in Chapter 1.

The small white box under the R in READY is called the *cursor.* Whenever the computer accepts letters from the keyboard, it uses this square to mark the spot where your next letter will be displayed. Type a letter—anything you want. It will appear where the cursor is, and the cursor will move to the right.

There are a few peculiarities of this keyboard that are worth noting. First of all, there are keys for the numbers 0 and 1. If you are used to a typewriter, you may be accustomed to using the letters O and L for these digits. You can't do this on the computer: you must give it numbers when it expects numbers.

Auto-repeat is another new feature. If you hold down any key more than a second, it will start to repeat. You could, if you wanted, type a string of Zs across the screen by merely holding down the Z key. The repeating will stop when you release the key. The auto-repeat feature is particularly useful with the space bar, at times when you want to move to the middle of a line.

If you make a mistake as you are typing, you can correct it with the

Figure 3.1: *The Atari 600XL keyboard.*

BACK SPACE key, at the upper-right corner of the keyboard. When you press this key, the cursor backs up one space to the left and deletes the letter in that space. You can then type the correct letter and continue as if nothing had happened.

As you type, you will notice that all of your letters are capitalized. The Atari computers can display lowercase letters, but in most cases, they require that your commands be capitalized. Because of this, the computer starts by using all caps.

If you want to type with lowercase letters, press the CAPS key, at the far right edge of the keyboard. The computer now reads the letters you type as lowercase. As with a typewriter, you can capitalize individual letters by pressing one of the SHIFT keys. To switch back into uppercase, press the CAPS key again. (On the Atari 400 and 800, you have to press the SHIFT and CAPS keys together to return to uppercase.) The SHIFT key does not "release" the CAPS lock, as it would on a typewriter.

To type symbols found on the upper half of the nonletter keys, you must use the SHIFT key, *even when you have the CAPS lock on.* These symbols include the exclamation point (!) and the quotation mark (").

You can use another special key to produce an interesting effect. Atari computers have an *inverse-video* key, which changes the appearance of the letters you type on the screen. This key, which looks like a square with a diagonal drawn through it (◪), is located next to the SHIFT key at the lower right of the keyboard on the Atari 600XL and 800XL. On the 1200XL, and the projected 1400XL and 1450XLD models, the inverse-video key is next to the BREAK key on the row of silver keys along the top. On the older Atari models 400 and 800, this key has the Atari logo ( ) on it, and is located next to the SHIFT at the lower right.

Try pressing the inverse-video key once. Then type some letters. They will appear on the screen as blue letters in a white box, rather than the standard white on blue. As you type, the white boxes join to form a solid white background. Once you have selected this inverse-video mode, you can type as you would in the normal mode, and switch between uppercase and lowercase in the usual way. To return to typing white on blue, press the inverse-video key a second time.

Figure 3.2 shows the four different styles of text you can display, using combinations of the inverse-video key and the CAPS key. The first line was typed just as the computer was turned on. All of the letters are capitalized and are displayed in normal video. For the second line, the CAPS key was pressed once. The isolated capital letters within the line were produced with the SHIFT key. Before the third line, the inverse-video and CAPS keys were pressed, to show how your text would look if you turned the computer on and switched immediately to inverse video. For the fourth line, the display was again put into lower-case with the CAPS key, but was left in inverse video.

Figure 3.2 also shows an important aspect of the Atari computer's keyboard and screen. The fourth example is longer than the 38 characters that will fit on the line. Rather than go off the right edge of the screen when a line is too long, the computer automatically drops down to the next line and continues. This is a nice feature, since it lets you type commands longer than a single line. At times, however, this can be somewhat unsightly, since words might be cut in the middle (like the word "low/er" in Figure 3.2).

If you're accustomed to an electric typewriter, you might be tempted to press the RETURN key at the end of a line you have typed. On the computer, however, the RETURN key has a special

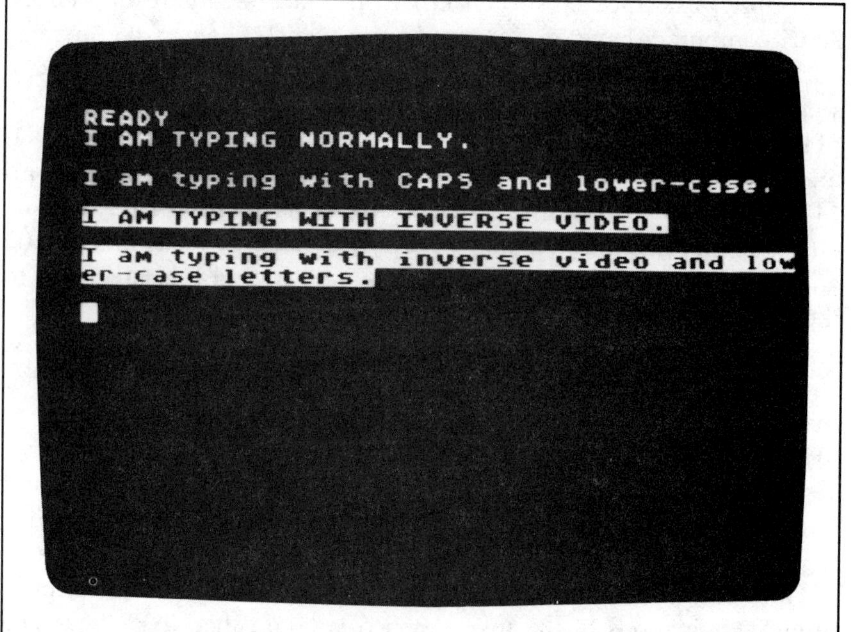

Figure 3.2: *Lower-case and inverse-video text on the screen.*

function: it enters the line as a command to the computer. So far, you haven't learned any commands, so you shouldn't use this key. If you do, your computer will print the word ERROR to show its disapproval.

For right now, use the BREAK key instead of the RETURN key to end each line. This tells the computer to drop down to the beginning of the next line on the screen, without responding to the line that you have just typed. On most Atari computers, you will find the BREAK key at the upper-right corner of the keyboard. On the 1200XL and 1400XL models, it lies at the right end of the line of silver keys along the top of the keyboard.

CONTROLLING THE CURSOR

You have seen that the letters you type are displayed on your television's screen. The letters appear from left to right, and the cursor slides to the right in front of them, showing where you are on the screen.

You aren't locked into this left-to-right motion, however. You will often want to use *editing* commands to control what happens on the screen. With certain keys and key combinations, you can move the cursor anywhere you choose on the screen, and even go back to correct letters you have already typed.

As you remember, the cursor shows where the next letter you type will be displayed. If you move the cursor to another place, you can type your next letter there. If you then continue typing, the letters will resume their left-to-right motion from the place you've moved to.

To move the cursor, you will need to use the CONTROL key, located just above the SHIFT on the left side of the keyboard. The CONTROL key has no meaning by itself, but is always used with another key. To use one of these special commands, press and hold the CONTROL key. As long as you hold it down, the computer will interpret the rest of the keyboard as commands, rather than as letters. To give the command, press the specific key that you want to use.

(If you press CONTROL with one of the letters of the alphabet, the computer will display a special *graphics character.* These can be used to create pictures on the screen, but are rather difficult to use. This book will not treat the graphics characters, but you are free to experiment with them.)

The most important of these special commands are the four arrow keys located to the right of the letters on the keyboard. These arrows move the cursor around the screen. The left arrow, for example, will move it back one space; the down arrow will move it one line straight down. When you move the cursor with the arrow keys, it passes over letters you have typed without changing them; it merely highlights them to show you where it is. You can move the cursor rapidly by holding down the arrow key. If you try to move the cursor off the edge of the screen, it will reappear on the other side.

The left arrow, located on the plus key, is the most useful of the four. To use it, you must press the plus key, while holding the control key down. Note that the plus key serves three different purposes. Typed alone, it is a plus sign (+). Typed with the SHIFT key, it is a backwards slash (\ ). Typed with the CONTROL key, as described here, it tells the computer to move the cursor one space to the left.

The four arrow keys will enable you to move the cursor anywhere on the screen. You could, for example, use the arrow keys to move to the bottom of the screen and type a message there, as in Figure 3.3.

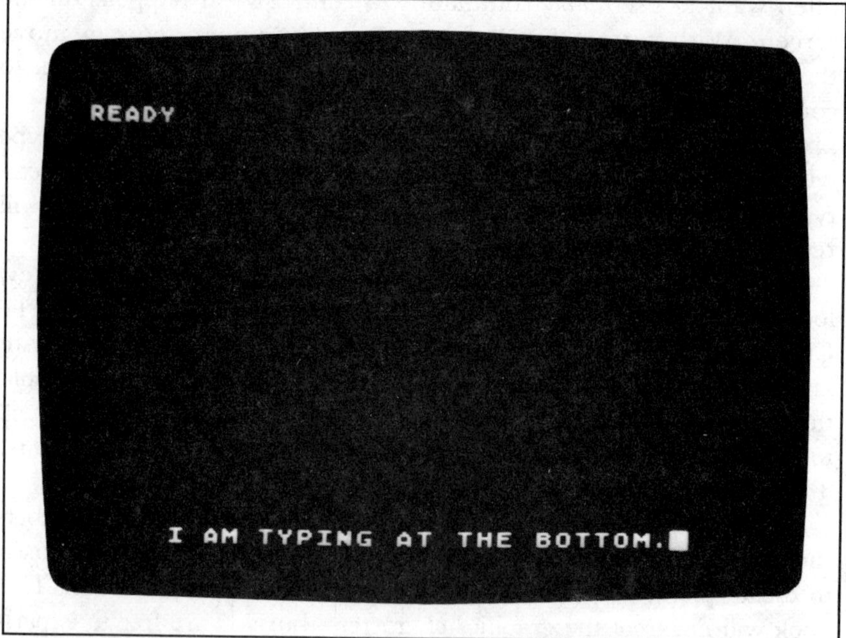

Figure 3.3: *The arrow keys let you type on other parts of the screen.*

To see the arrow keys in action, type the following line on the screen:

THIS LINE CONTAINS A MESTAKE

Press CONTROL and the left arrow key six times so that the cursor is over the E. Then release the control key and type an I. The I replaces the E and corrects the misspelled word.

This sort of correction is very useful. Unless you are a perfect typist, you will certainly make mistakes from time to time. You can, it is true, retype the line from the beginning, but in most cases you will find it easier to move the cursor back and just correct the error.

What if you leave a letter out? Suppose you have typed this instead:

THIS LINE CONTAINS A MSTAKE

If you simply back up and type the missing I, it will appear on the screen, but will replace a letter that you wanted. To avoid this, use the INSERT command, located on the > key at the upper right of the keyboard. Move the cursor back with the left-arrow key, until it is over the S. Then hold the CONTROL key down and press INSERT. The S and the letters following will move one space to the right, opening up the space covered by the cursor. Now you can type the I into that space, and the correction is complete. When you need to insert more than one letter, press the INSERT key several times.

You have already used the DELETE/BACK SPACE key to erase mistakes. This key, when used in combination with CONTROL or SHIFT, has two other meanings as well, which allow you to delete letters in other ways.

To remove extra letters from the middle of a line without leaving a space, use DELETE/BACK SPACE with the CONTROL key. This combination deletes the letter covered by the cursor and closes up the space in the line. To see how this works, type yet another misspelled line:

THIS LINE CONTAINS A MISSTAKE

Now back the cursor up with CONTROL and the left-arrow key until it is over one of the S's in MISSTAKE. Hold down the CONTROL key and press DELETE. The extra S will disappear and the "TAKE" will move over to fill in the space. Note the differences between this and the simple BACK SPACE command: BACK SPACE would have moved the cursor back and deleted the letter to the left, and would have left a space in the line.

If you use SHIFT rather than CONTROL with the DELETE/ BACK SPACE key, you will delete the entire line you are on. This is very useful, if you need to clear unnecessary lines off the screen. You must be very careful, however, not to delete an entire line with SHIFT-DELETE when you meant to use CONTROL-DELETE or a simple BACK SPACE.

To the other side of the INSERT key is a key marked CLEAR, which lets you erase the entire screen. To use this function, hold down the CONTROL key and press CLEAR. All the letters on the screen will be erased, and the cursor will return to the upper left. You can use this command to clear the slate anytime the screen has become too cluttered for your taste. With some of the examples in this book, I will ask you to type CONTROL-CLEAR before you give a command. If you don't do this, you won't be able to make your screen match the figures I describe.

Figure 3.4 reviews the six editing controls. Practice them as you work through the pages that follow. You will soon find it easy to correct mistakes anywhere on the screen.

We have now covered most of the important keys on the Atari keyboard. We can use type text, move the cursor, and make corrections on the screen, using the Atari editing keys. We have avoided one key—RETURN—because it has a very special purpose. Let's turn to it now.

KEY	FUNCTION
BACK SPACE by itself	Erases your last character, and lets you type it over.
CONTROL + An arrow key	Moves the cursor.
CONTROL + INSERT	Adds a space in a line.
CONTROL + DELETE/BACK SPACE	Removes a space from a line.
SHIFT + DELETE/BACK SPACE	Erases the entire line.
CONTROL + CLEAR	Erases the entire screen.

Figure 3.4: *The keys for editing the screen.*

RETURN *AND THE ERROR MESSAGE*

Type a line of text such as the first line of Figure 3.5. Then press the RETURN key. You will get an ERROR message, as shown.

What is happening here? The RETURN key has a special function. It tells the computer to take the line you have typed and read it as a command. If it can understand the command, the computer will follow it. If it cannot understand, the computer assumes you have done something wrong, and prints an ERROR message.

You might object that your line made perfect sense. I agree, but the machine does not. Computers require that you do things exactly the way they want. Most English sentences do not fit within the computer's limited experience. Later in this chapter, you will learn some commands that do mean something to the machine.

Don't be put off by the word ERROR. It is merely the computer's way of saying it couldn't understand what you did. In this case, for instance, we typed something that made perfect sense to us, but not to the computer. The ERROR was its fault, not ours.

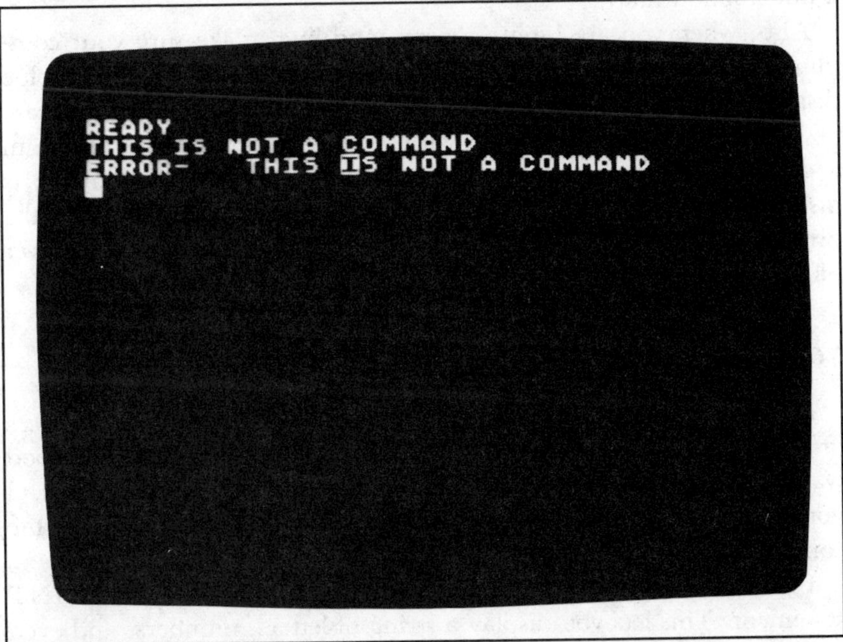

Figure 3.5: *You get an ERROR if you type a line the computer can't understand as a command.*

ERRORs are part of the natural course of mastering your computer, and you shouldn't be ashamed if you get a few. Your computer is *very* literal, and not at all forgiving. It will understand what you're saying only if you put it in *exactly* the form it requires. If you miss by even a comma, the computer will not understand you.

The computer will usually help you find your mistake by putting an inverse-video box around the first letter it can't understand. Your mistake will usually be to the left of this mark. At times, the computer will display an *error code* such as this:

```
ERROR-- 3
```

If you get one of these codes, you can look it up in Appendix C of this book. The code number 3 represents a *value error,* which means you probably used an illegal number somewhere in your command.

As you type the lines in this book, make sure that you copy them exactly as they are printed, right down to the last quotation mark. If you get an ERROR on any line you type, check it letter by letter against what's printed here: you might have misspelled a word or lost a punctuation mark.

Also, when you are typing a command line, make sure your computer is set for all capital letters, and is in its normal white-on-blue display mode. If your letters are showing on the screen as lowercase or inverse video, the computer will not be able to understand them in a command. There is only one exception to this rule, and it is discussed below. If you're not sure whether your computer is in the proper mode for commands, press the RESET key or turn the power off and back on.

YOUR FIRST COMMAND: ***PRINT***

So far, you have just been typing words and letters at various places on the screen, using your computer like a memo pad. This is a good way to learn about the keyboard, but it doesn't really help you control your computer. To do that, you will need to use a command that the computer can understand.

In this section, you will learn your first command: the PRINT statement. This lets you display a string of letters, numbers, and even the results of calculations on the screen. For right now, you will only use it to have the computer retype words and phrases, but later, you will be able to use it in many different ways. By trying these simple experiments with PRINT, you will also learn what a command is, and how it affects the computer.

To give a command, you type a line on the screen and press the RETURN key. The computer will then read the line you typed and try to follow its instructions. If it can't make sense of the line, the computer will give you an ERROR message.

Type the following line, just as it is:

```
PRINT "HELLO"
```

Then press the RETURN key. The computer should respond HELLO, as shown in Figure 3.6. (If you get an ERROR message when you press the RETURN key, you have probably made a typing mistake. Check to make sure you spelled PRINT correctly and put the quotation marks both before and after HELLO.)

You have typed your first command! The computer recognizes PRINT as a *keyword* with a special meaning. When the computer sees this word, it knows to search through the rest of the line and print

Figure 3.6: *How the computer should react to your first command.*

the message enclosed in quotes. It finds the word HELLO, so that is the message it displays. Note that the computer does not reproduce the quotation marks: they are merely a sign that the word HELLO is the message to be printed. After displaying the message, the computer then adds the word READY, to show it has finished and can accept another command.

The results may not be impressive, but you have made an important step with your first command. You have asked the computer to do something, in a way that it could understand. It read your command and displayed the results on the screen. With this step, you have begun to control your computer.

You can try many variations on this simple PRINT statement. You can put anything you want between the quotation marks and it will be printed exactly as you typed it. You can also use lowercase and inverse-video letters within the quotation marks (but nowhere else in the command). Also, any spaces you include between the quotes will be included in the message the computer prints. Figure 3.7 shows some of the things you can do.

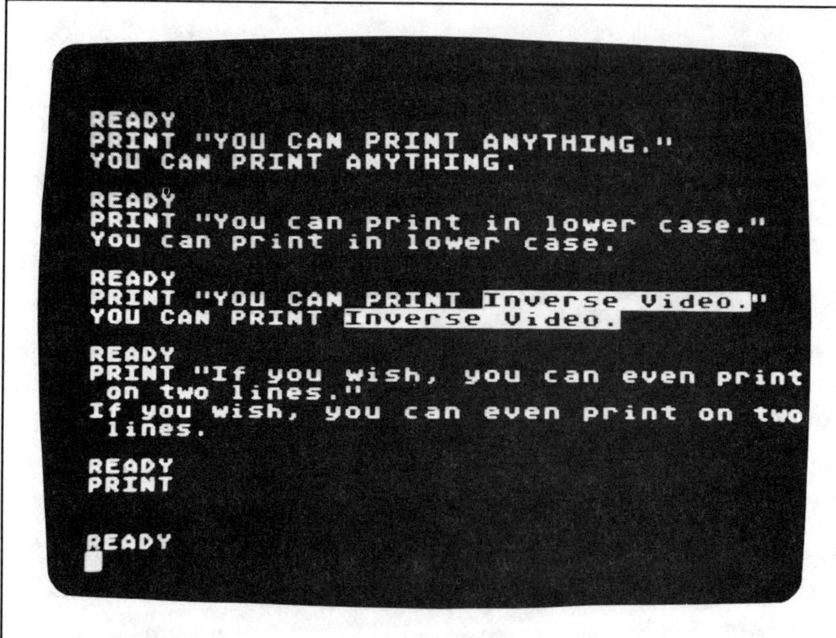

Figure 3.7: *Some examples of the PRINT statement.*

As you retype your variations on the basic PRINT statement, you can practice your editing skills. Use CONTROL-↑ to move the cursor up to one of the PRINT statements on the screen. Change or add something inside the quotation marks, then press RETURN. Your edited statement will be run again, and the computer will print the new text over the old one.

This illustrates a useful aspect of your computer's screen display. Any line that is still on the screen is "live" and can be used again. All you need to do is move the cursor back to the line you want to reuse, make your change, and press RETURN—the cursor may be anywhere on the line. The computer will run the line again exactly as it appears on the screen. Any changes you have made will be carried into effect.

This is especially useful if you get an ERROR on a long command. Instead of typing it all over again, move the cursor back up and correct the mistake in the line. You can then press RETURN and reuse the line.

The fourth PRINT statement in Figure 3.7 runs across more than one line. That is fine, as long as you type the entire command as a unit, without pressing BREAK or RETURN. If you haven't finished your message when the cursor reaches the edge of the screen, just keep typing: the computer automatically goes onto the next line down. You can type commands as long as three full lines of text. The computer will warn you with a beep when you approach the limit.

The last line of Figure 3.7 shows an important use of the PRINT command. If you type PRINT, but do not give any message, the computer will print a blank line on the screen (actually two, if you count the one that automatically appears above the word READY).

It is possible to give more than one command at a time. Instead of pressing RETURN at the end of the first command, type a colon (:). Then type your second command. In this way, you can add as many commands as will fit within the limit of three lines on the screen. When you're done, press RETURN and all of the commands will be carried out in sequence.

Figure 3.8 shows how you can use blank lines and multiple statements together to improve the appearance of your screen display. The command begins with three simple PRINT statements, with no message, to put three blank lines on the screen. The fourth PRINT in the command has a message, which begins with twelve spaces so that it will be centered on the screen. A fifth PRINT adds a second line, starting five spaces in from the left. A final PRINT puts an extra blank line on the screen between the message and the word READY that will appear.

The PRINT statement is one of the most important commands you will learn. No matter how deeply you explore your computer, you will always need to display the results on the screen. With the PRINT statement, you can do this in any way you wish.

*THE **ESC** KEY*

The way we have been doing things, the screen remains cluttered with your PRINT statement when your message is displayed. Suppose you want to have only your message left on the screen when you're done. You might be tempted to type the CONTROL-CLEAR function as part of your message, something like this:

```
PRINT "{CONTROL-CLEAR} HELLO"
```

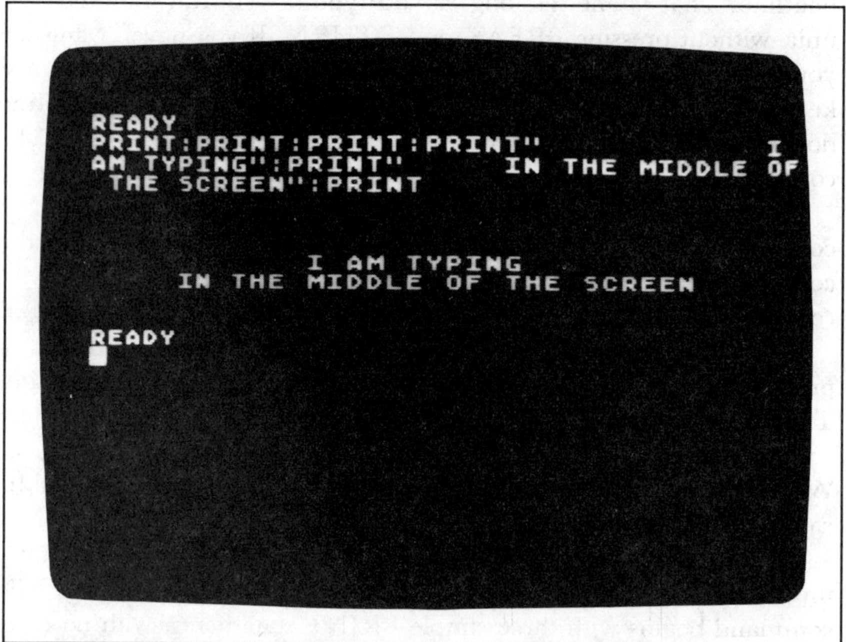

Figure 3.8: *Blank lines and multiple PRINT statements can make your screen more readable.*

Unfortunately, this doesn't work. The computer will clear the screen as soon as you press CONTROL-CLEAR, and you will never get a chance to complete the command with the message HELLO.

What we want is a way to store the CONTROL-CLEAR function as part of the printed message. If you could do this, you could have the computer wait to clear the screen until you have finished typing the command. Then, when you finally press the RETURN key, it would use the stored CONTROL-CLEAR function just before it actually displays the message.

To do this, you can use the ESC key, located in the upper-left corner of the keyboard. ESC stands for "escape," and is used to delay the effect of the next control character you type in a PRINT statement.

Let's try using the ESC key to PRINT the word HELLO on a blank screen. Type the word PRINT and an opening quotation mark. Then press the ESC key once. It will look as if nothing has happened, since the ESC key itself is not displayed. Now press CONTROL-CLEAR. Instead of erasing the screen immediately, the computer will display a curved arrow in a white box. This symbol shows that CONTROL-CLEAR has been stored as part of the line, to be used when the message is displayed. Finish typing the message with the word HELLO and the closing quote, so that your command looks like Figure 3.9.

Now press the RETURN key. The computer will print the message HELLO, but before it does, it will clear the screen. Figure 3.10 shows the result. This greeting is much more readable than Figure 3.6, in which the PRINT statement was left on the screen.

CONTROL-CLEAR has actually become a character that is part of the message. When the computer PRINTs the stored character, it acts as if you had just typed it at the point where it appears in the message. Any words you included in the message after the CONTROL-CLEAR will be printed after the screen is cleared, not before.

Note that you have to type the ESC-CONTROL-CLEAR as part of the message enclosed within the quotation marks. If you put the ESC-CONTROL-CLEAR anywhere outside the quotes, you will get an ERROR.

The ESC key can be used to delay the effect of any CONTROL key in a PRINT command. By storing combinations of the four arrow keys, for instance, you can have the computer position text anywhere on the screen. Each time the computer encounters a stored arrow key, it will move a space in that direction before it continues to print the line.

Figure 3.11 shows an example that stores the down arrow in this way. Type the PRINT statement exactly as it is shown at the top of the screen. Wherever you see the ↓ symbol, type ESC and then CONTROL-↓.

When you press the RETURN key at the end of the line, the computer will print the message within the quotation marks, exactly as you stored it. The first thing it sees is the stored down arrow. This causes it to drop down a line before it displays the word UPPER. After that, it encounters two more down arrows. These cause the computer to drop two lines further down before it prints the word LOWER. You could have achieved the same effect by using four separate PRINT statements, but it would have been much more complicated. These ESC and CONTROL characters let you position your messages much more easily.

Figure 3.9: *Use the ESC key to store a control character in a line you're printing.*

THE SPECIAL FUNCTION KEYS

You might be wondering about the special keys such as START, OPTION, SELECT, and HELP. On the Atari 600XL and 800XL, these are square silver buttons to the right of the keyboard. On the 1200XL, 1400XL, and 1450XLD, these keys are spread across the silver strip just above the keyboard. On the older Atari computers, the special keys are large yellow buttons along the right side of the keyboard.

Unless you become an advanced programmer, you will use these keys only when you are running programs you buy in the store. Many of Atari's games use the START, OPTION, and SELECT keys as one-button commands to replay, change the level of difficulty, or change the style of play. You will also use the OPTION key if you need to disable the BASIC language as you load certain diskette programs. While it is possible to incorporate these keys into programs you write, the procedure is too technical for this book.

HELP is a new key that Atari added when it redesigned its line of

Figure 3.10: *ESC-CONTROL-CLEAR gives you a clean screen before you PRINT.*

computers. At the moment, few programs are available that use this key, but some are being planned.

The Atari 1200XL and 1400XL computers also have four *programmable function keys,* labeled F1 through F4. These can be programmed in the same way as the START, OPTION, and SELECT keys, but the subject is, once again, rather technical.

The RESET key is the last of this group. Chapter 1 mentioned this key as a kind of panic button that lets you regain control of your computer when you don't know what it is doing. When you press the RESET key, the computer stops whatever it was doing and switches itself back to the state it was in when you first turned on the power.

As a "start-over" function, the RESET key is very useful. In the following chapters, we will often do things that alter the screen display or put the computer into strange modes. Rather than worry about giving commands to make the computer return to its accustomed manners, it is often easier to press the RESET key. The screen will revert to its familiar blue, and READY will appear in the corner.

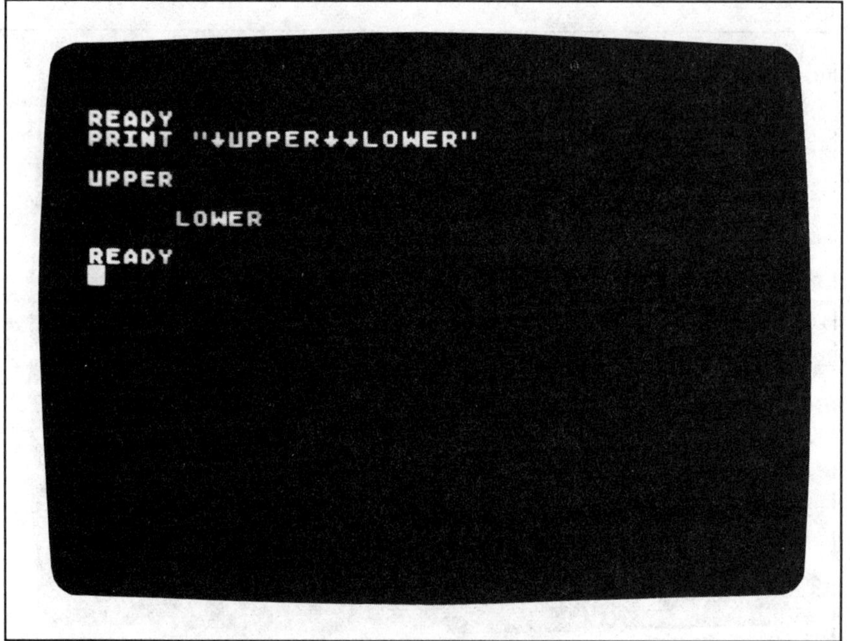

Figure 3.11: *By storing down arrows in a PRINT statement, you can display text on more than one line.*

RESET, however, is a rather drastic step. It stops everything and cancels many of the things you have done. That may be what you wanted, but you should be sure before you press it. Be especially careful when you have a program stored in the computer's memory: the RESET key can erase parts of long programs.

OPTIONAL EXERCISES

Now that you have finished this introduction to your computer's keyboard and screen, you might want to try your own hand at some exercises. These are *optional,* food for thought and avenues for further exploration. I hope you'll try them, but you won't need to have done them to read further in this book. Answers are provided after the Appendices in the back of this book.

1. Use the arrow keys to type block letters made up of asterisks (*) on the screen. Move the cursor around and put asterisks in the places where you want them to go. Remember to use only the arrow keys as you do this: you will spoil your picture with an ERROR if you press RETURN.
2. On page 39, we saw a way to put more than one PRINT statement in a single command, separated by colons (:). Use three PRINT statements to produce the following message:

   ```
   ONE
   TWO
   THREE
   ```

   Can you achieve a similar result in a single PRINT statement, using ESC and the arrow keys?
3. Replace the down arrows in Figure 3.11 with up arrows. What happens when you press RETURN? Why does the computer print the word READY right on top of the statement?

SUMMARY

The keyboard and the screen work together. With the keyboard, you can type letters and numbers that appear directly on the screen.

You can also type CONTROL characters that move the cursor or change the screen. You can use these CONTROL keys to edit the lines you have typed, to insert and delete characters, or to clear the screen.

With the PRINT statement, you can ask the computer to display messages on the screen. You can even store control characters in the message, using the ESC key, so that the computer will clear the screen before printing your message, or move the message elsewhere on the screen.

You have covered a lot of ground in this chapter. You have learned everything you need to know to use your computer's keyboard, and you know how the computer controls the screen. Most important, you have given your first command, and the computer gave its response. In the pages ahead, we will cover many other commands that will increase your control of your computer.

CHAPTER FOUR

Atari Graphics

If you have played Pac-Man or any other video game, you know that your computer can display more than just letters and numbers on your television screen. It can draw very colorful pictures, with impressive animation effects.

In this chapter, you will learn about your computer's graphic display system. You will learn how to use coordinates, and how to plot points on the screen. With a few simple commands, you will be able to display letters, choose colors, and draw pictures.

The Atari computer has 16 different modes for displaying text and graphics. This chapter gives an overview of all of them, then covers two in detail. The other modes will be discussed in Chapter 8.

Graphics are one of the most appealing features of your Atari computer. I hope you will enjoy them.

WHAT ARE GRAPHICS?

The word *graphics* refers to any type of display you can put on the screen other than plain text. This could mean a picture, such as a box or a cube. It could be a bar or line graph, such as those used to show the state of the economy. Or it could be an animated game, such as Pac-Man.

Of the computer's 16 graphics modes, 5 are called *text modes,* because they are used to type letters rather than draw lines. You have already seen one kind of text, the letters you have been typing on the screen. The other four text modes shape their letters in different ways and let you control the colors of individual letters. Using these other text modes is somewhat complicated, however, so I will not describe them until Chapter 8.

The other eleven are true *graphics modes*. All of them work on the same principle: you can plot points individually or draw lines in any direction across the screen. The modes differ in the number of colors, and in the degree of detail, or *resolution,* available to you.

Why all these modes? Atari has realized that you will want to have different features for different tasks. For a bar graph, you will want to have thick lines, with relatively little detail. For an intricate picture, you will want to draw with fine lines, and show lots of detail. By choosing different graphics modes, you can get just the amount of detail you want.

Another reason for having different modes involves the computer's memory. When you ask the computer to use very high resolution and many colors, it will need a lot of its memory to store the picture. If you have one of the more expensive Atari computers or a memory expansion, this is no great problem: even at the highest resolution, the picture will only use a fraction of the memory. If you have only the basic Atari 600XL, however, high-resolution graphics will use up more than half of the available space. This might cause problems if you are writing a complicated program. (With the programs in this book, however, you don't need to worry about running out of memory space. All of them will work on an unexpanded 600XL.)

So, your Atari computer lets you choose exactly the combination of features you need. If you need four colors and high resolution, you can choose that. If you don't, you can save memory space by choosing one of the modes with less detail or fewer colors.

For simplicity, this chapter will cover only two of the sixteen modes available. The first is the normal text mode, which you have already been using. The other is mode 7, *four-color graphics,* which lets you plot detailed pictures on the screen.

These are the most important of the sixteen modes, and they will serve well for everything in this book. Chapter 8 discusses the other modes, and gives some examples of what you can do with them.

TEXT: ***GRAPHICS 0***

This is the mode you've been using so far. When you turn the computer on, it is automatically set up for this kind of text, so you don't need to do anything special. At other times, however, you may want to switch back into normal text from another graphics mode, so you should know how to do it.

You switch graphics modes by typing the word GRAPHICS, followed by the number of the mode. The normal text mode is number 0, so you would type this:

```
GRAPHICS 0
```

Like the PRINT statement, this is a command, so you'll need to press RETURN after you've finished. If you do this now, the screen will just flash and say READY again: you're just switching from mode 0 to mode 0. Later on, you will type this when you want to get out of the other graphics modes and return to plain text.

Let's start by reviewing what we know about the text mode:

- With the PRINT statement, we can ask the computer to display any message we put within quotation marks. Unless we tell it to do something different, the computer will display the message on the next line after the PRINT command on the screen.
- By typing ESC-CONTROL-CLEAR at the beginning of the text within the quotation marks of the PRINT statement, we can have the computer clear the screen before it displays the message.
- By typing ESC, CONTROL, and an arrow key within the PRINT statement message, we can ask the computer to move to another part of the screen before it types the message. It is also possible to space downward by PRINTing blank lines, but this is rather cumbersome.

*THE **POSITION** STATEMENT*

With the commands you have already learned, you can display a message anywhere you choose on the screen. You have probably found it rather difficult to do this, though, because you had to use repeated ESC and CONTROL key combinations to move around the screen. For this reason, Atari has given you another command: the POSITION statement. This lets you move directly to any place on the screen, before you start to PRINT your text.

When you use the POSITION statement, you name the row and column you want to move to. The computer thinks of the screen as a grid 40 columns wide and 24 rows high, as shown in Figure 4.1. Each row and column is given a number. The columns are numbered 0 to 39, from left to right, and the rows are numbered 0 to 23, from top to bottom.

With this numbering system, you can name any point in the grid with a pair of numbers. With the first number, you choose the column, to tell the computer how far to move in from the left edge of the screen. With the second number, you pick the row, to say how far you want to go down from the top of the screen. The point you choose will be the box where that row and that column meet.

These two numbers are called the point's *coordinates.* The first number always names the column, or the distance over from the left. This number is often called the *x-coordinate.* The second number always represents the row, or the distance down from the top; it is called the *y-coordinate.* Programs in this book will often use the letters X and Y to refer to horizontal and vertical locations. You can think of the pair of numbers as "X spaces over and Y spaces down."

Figure 4.2 shows the coordinates of some points on the screen. The square in the upper-left corner is always 0,0—0 spaces over and 0

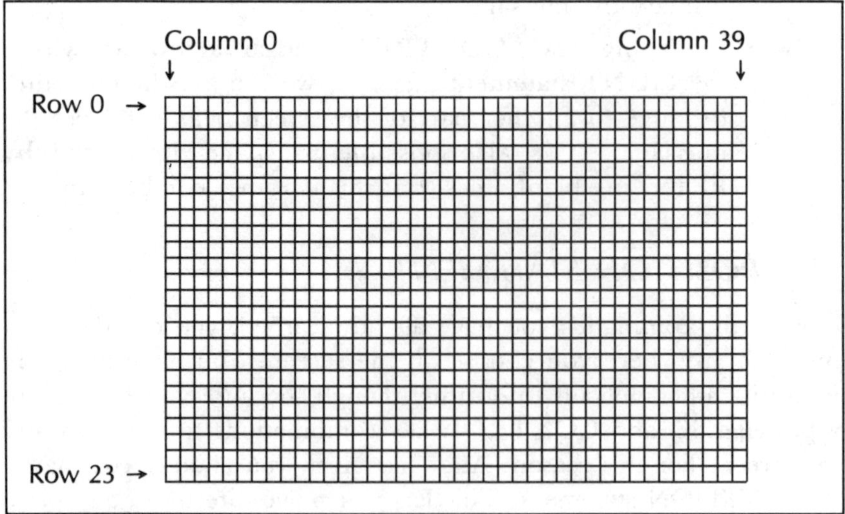

Figure 4.1: *The Atari computer lays its screen out like a grid.*

spaces down. This is true in the numbering system of every Atari graphics mode. For the box at the upper-right corner, you need to count all the way over to the 39th column from the left. Thus, the x-coordinate of this point is 39. The y-coordinate remains 0, because you didn't move any spaces down. We therefore write '39,0', meaning "39 over and 0 down." For the point at the lower-left corner, you move 0 spaces over and 23 spaces down, so its coordinates are 0,23. To reach the point at the lower right, you move all the way over and all the way down; its coordinates are therefore 39,23.

To name the point in the center of the screen, we need to do some figuring. For the x-coordinate, we need to choose a number roughly halfway between 0 and 39. This could be either 19 or 20, but we'll choose 19 so that we don't crowd the right-hand side of the screen. Likewise, we need a value about halfway down the vertical scale of 0 to 23, so we'll choose 11. These coordinates (19,11) select the box shown in the middle of Figure 4.2: it is 19 spaces over and 11 spaces down.

The POSITION statement lets you move to any coordinates on the screen. If you follow this with a PRINT command, the message will start at the point you have moved to.

If the coordinates happen to be on a line that already contains text,

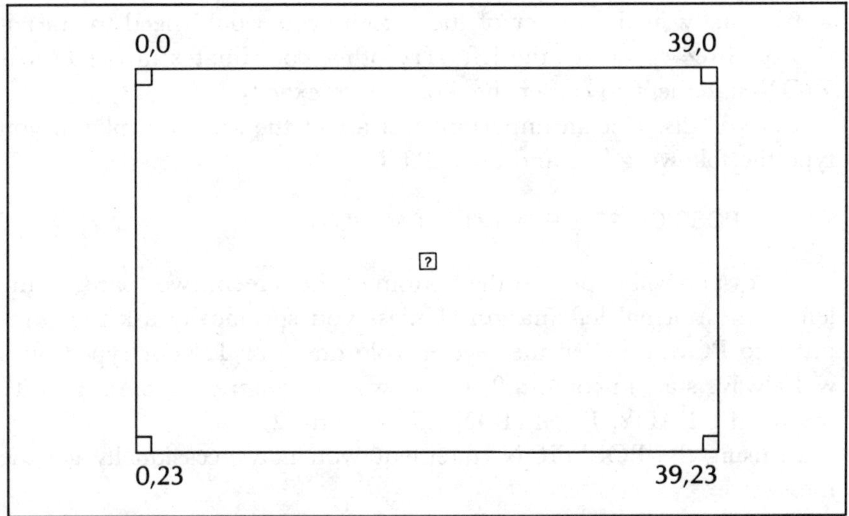

Figure 4.2: *Some sample coordinates in the GRAPHICS 0 (text) mode.*

the new message will be printed on top of what is already there. Since that may be hard to read, it is often best to press CONTROL/ CLEAR before you give a POSITION command. If you don't do this, you may not be able to see what the particular command has done, and your television screen will not match the figures in this book.

Now that you understand coordinates, the POSITION statement is very simple. To move to the point in the center of the screen, simply type:

```
POSITION 19,11
```

If you press RETURN now, the computer will move the cursor to these coordinates. But since you didn't give it anything to PRINT at that point, it immediately moves on and displays the READY message on the following line. The cursor then appears below that to await your next entry. Now clear the screen and type:

```
POSITION 19,11: PRINT "CENTER"
```

Then press RETURN, and your screen should look like Figure 4.3.

The displayed word appears a little to the right of center on the screen. This is because the POSITION statement sets the place only for the beginning of the word. The C in CENTER appears in the box (19,11); the word, however, continues on to the right. To place the word exactly in the center of the screen, you would need to start it two or three spaces to the left. Try other coordinates in the POSITION statement to center the word more exactly.

You will discover an important fact about the screen display if you type the following line and press RETURN:

```
POSITION 20,0: PRINT "LEFT MARGIN"
```

The message will appear at the bottom of the screen, two spaces to the left of the normal left margin. Unless you specifically ask the computer to POSITION a message in columns 0 or 1, your typed lines will always start in column 2. If you want to align your message with the word READY, POSITION it in column 2.

In using the POSITION statement, you may occasionally get the message

```
ERROR-- 141
```

If you look up this error code in Appendix C, you will see that this means "Cursor out of range." This means that you tried to move to a point that was off the screen—one of your coordinates was too large. Remember, the maximums for the X and Y coordinates are 39 and 23, respectively. When you get an ERROR, just CLEAR the screen and start over.

Experiment with the POSITION statement and the layout of the coordinates. You will find it useful to think in terms of coordinates as you start to use graphics. While the numbers of rows and columns are different in the other graphics modes, the basic idea remains the same.

FOUR-COLOR DRAWING: ***GRAPHICS 7***

So far, we've only been working with letters. Now we're going to do some real graphics, drawing pictures on the screen. In the remainder of this chapter, you will learn how to plot points, draw lines, and make pictures on the screen.

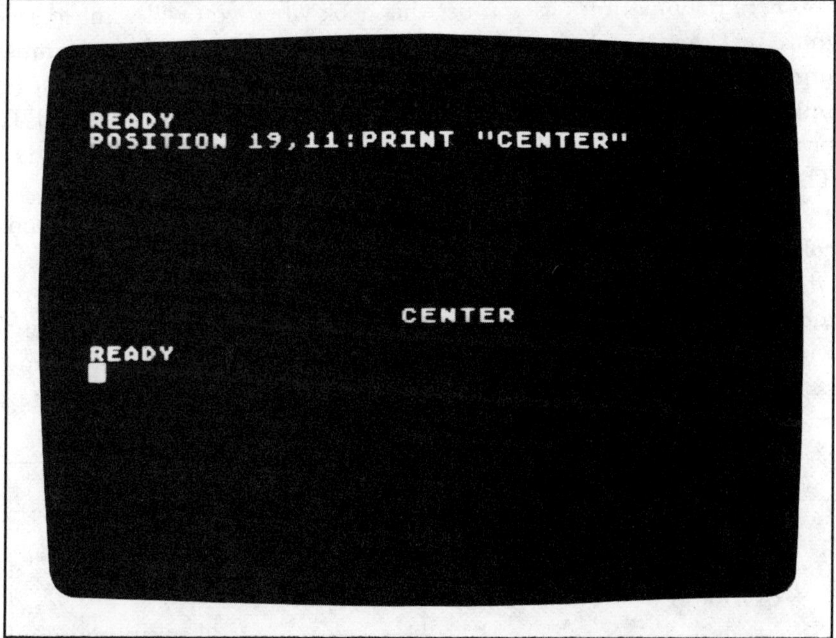

Figure 4.3: *Use the POSITION statement to display messages where you want them on the screen.*

To draw pictures, we will be using graphics mode 7, one of the *four-color graphics* modes. Don't worry about the modes that come between 0 and 7: we'll talk about them later.

To get into four-color graphics, type

```
GRAPHICS 7
```

and press RETURN. The top part of the screen will turn black and the word READY will appear at the bottom.

The black part of the screen is devoted to the graphic designs you are about to draw. You cannot move the cursor into this region, and you cannot PRINT messages there, but you can use it to draw pictures using points and lines. This region is called the *graphics screen.*

The graphics do not reach all the way to the bottom of the screen, because the computer has to leave you some room to enter commands and PRINT messages. These bottom four lines, where the words remain, are called the *text window.* In Chapter 8, you will learn a way to extend the graphics down into this part of the screen as well. For now, however, you'll need the text window to keep track of what you type.

There may be times as you use this book when you will want to see more text than can fit in the text window. Especially in the programming chapters, you may often want to look at an extended text that is much too long for these four lines. When this happens, press RESET or type a GRAPHICS 0 command to return to the normal text mode. Then you can display the extended text on a full screen once again.

Your computer gives you four *paintbrushes* in this mode, one for each color. Three of the four are drawing colors (orange, green, and blue), while the fourth is an *erasebrush,* which you will use to clear points from the screen. The erasebrush is actually a black paintbrush, drawing with the background color: when you paint a point black, it disappears. It is possible to change the brushes to colors other than orange,

PAINTBRUSH NUMBER	PRESET COLOR
COLOR 1	Orange
COLOR 2	Green
COLOR 3	Blue
COLOR 0	Erase (= black background)

Figure 4.4: *The colors of the four paintbrushes.*

green, blue, and black, but for the moment these will suffice.

Before you start drawing, you must choose which of the paintbrushes you wish to use. You do this by giving a COLOR command, such as:

```
COLOR 1
```

This chooses paintbrush number 1, which is preset to orange. Figure 4.4 shows the colors of each of the paintbrushes.

Figure 4.5 shows the layout of the four-color graphics screen. The top part of the screen is divided into a fine grid 160 dots wide and 80 dots high. You can refer to any dot on this grid by naming a pair of numbers as coordinates. The graphics coordinates follow the same system as the coordinates in the text mode, except that there are more rows and columns. In this mode, the x-coordinate runs from 0 to 159 and the y-coordinate from 0 to 79. Figure 4.5 shows the coordinates you would use to plot the points in each corner of the graphics screen.

You can display either points or lines on the graphics screen, using two commands. With PLOT, you can light up a single point on the graphics screen. With DRAWTO, you can display a straight line between two points.

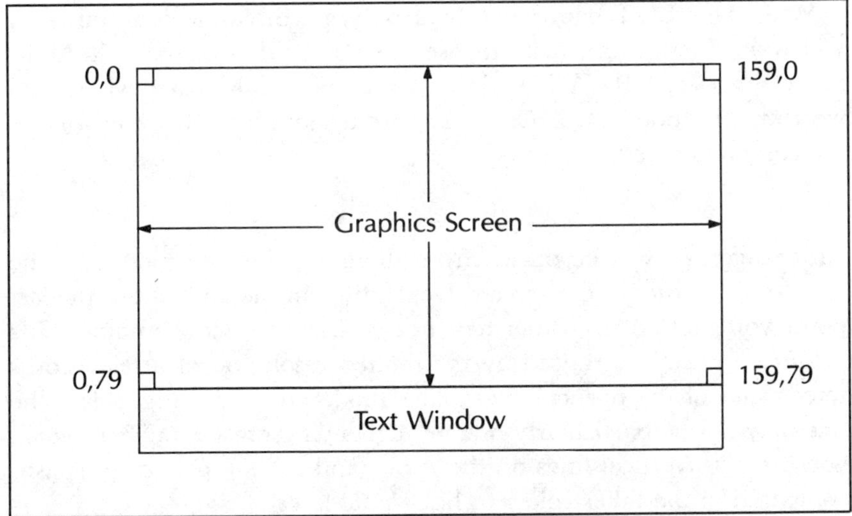

Figure 4.5: *The layout of the four-color graphics screen.*

Generally, you will want to PLOT a point first. To do this, choose the orange paintbrush, by typing

```
COLOR 1
```

Then type a line such as this:

```
PLOT 10,20
```

A pinpoint of light should appear in the upper-left corner of the screen. If it didn't, check to make sure you have given the command GRAPHICS 7, and that you have given a COLOR command to choose a paintbrush. Also, make sure that your television is tuned well enough that you can see this small point: it's finer than a period.

The '10,20' in the PLOT statement named the coordinates of the point: 10 units over from the left, 20 units down from the top. These are relatively small movements on the 160 × 80-square grid of the graphics coordinates; if you want to see how small, PLOT the point 0,0. Note that this would have been quite a large distance in the normal text mode. Graphics grids tend to be finer than text grids.

You can PLOT as many points as you wish on the screen. Try a few, to get a feel for the graphics coordinates. Each PLOT command will result in another single point, provided you didn't exceed the limits (159 for the x-coordinate, 79 for the y). If you do give a bad number, you will get an error message, but you can continue typing.

With the PLOT command, you only get disconnected points. If you want lines, you'll need to use the DRAWTO command. As its name suggests, DRAWTO connects a line from the place where you were, to the point you name as your destination. Try the following command:

```
DRAWTO 159,79
```

An orange line will be drawn from the last point you plotted to the lower-right corner of the screen. Depending on the angle from the last point you plotted, the line may not look exactly continuous. This "staircase effect" is caused by the limited resolution of a television's screen and of the particular graphics mode you are using. Also, the line may not be particularly orange, depending on the angle at which you drew it. Vertical lines on the Atari tend to look pale or purplish, compared to the fuller colors of horizontal lines.

PLOT and DRAWTO work hand in hand. To draw a line, you

will generally first use a PLOT command to display the starting point of the line. Then, you'll use a DRAWTO command to draw the line to its ending point. If you start right off with a DRAWTO command, without first plotting a starting point, the computer will start the line from the coordinates last used.

As an example, let's draw a horizontal line across the screen. Type the following two commands:

```
PLOT 0,20
DRAWTO 159,20
```

After the first command, a point will appear a third of the way down the left edge of the screen. With the second command, your computer will draw a straight orange line across to the right side.

Suppose you want to draw a green line just below this. You will need to change to paintbrush 2, then draw the other line. The following three commands will do this:

```
COLOR 2
PLOT 0,30
DRAWTO 159,30
```

Note that the Y (vertical) coordinate has been changed to move the line further down. How would you plot a blue line just below the green?

If you give another DRAWTO command, the computer will continue the new line from the endpoint of the last one. A series of DRAWTO commands is like drawing a number of straight lines on a paper without lifting your pencil. There is no need to give a new PLOT command to start each new segment. If, on the other hand, you want to lift your paintbrush and start a new line not connected to the rest, you will need to PLOT the starting point of the new line. Think of it this way: DRAWTO traces a line from your present position to your next point, while PLOT moves the paintbrush without tracing a line.

To see these concepts in action, let's draw the box shown in Figure 4.6. Start by clearing the screen and choosing paintbrush 1, with the lines:

```
GRAPHICS 7
COLOR 1
```

Then give the following five commands:

```
PLOT 10,10
DRAWTO 70,10
DRAWTO 70,70
DRAWTO 10,70
DRAWTO 10,10
```

With the PLOT command, a small point will appear near the upper-left corner of the screen. Each DRAWTO command adds an edge of the box, until the final one brings the paintbrush back to the starting point. Since the four sides of the box are connected, you didn't need to lift the brush with a PLOT command.

There are several ways you can erase portions of your screen. The simplest is to use the erasebrush, paintbrush 0, by typing

```
COLOR 0
```

When you do this, your PLOT and DRAWTO commands become

Figure 4.6: *Drawing a box on the screen.*

erase commands, until you choose another paintbrush. Try typing the following lines:

```
COLOR 0
PLOT 10,10
DRAWTO 70,10
```

The top of the box should disappear. (If it doesn't, you probably mistyped one of the coordinates. Try retyping the last two examples.)

If you want to erase the whole screen, however, the best thing to do is to type

```
GRAPHICS 7
```

This resets the screen and lets you start all over. You may need to type COLOR 1 again before you can start painting.

That brings us to the end of our introduction to Atari graphics. There is much more that you can do with your computer's graphics; we have only scratched the surface. Chapter 8 of this book describes briefly how you can use the 14 other graphics modes to produce varied effects. It will describe modes which allow you to use as many as 16 colors on the screen at once. It will explain *high-resolution graphics,* a one-color mode that lets you plot finer points than you can with four-color graphics. Finally, it will cover the *special-text* modes, which give you other ways to print text, including color. But this is enough for now.

OPTIONAL EXERCISES

1. Using three POSITION and three PRINT statements in one long command, display your name in three places on the screen. Try to picture where the words will appear before you press RETURN.
2. Rerun the commands you used to draw the orange box in Figure 4.6. Then give a second series of commands, to draw a blue box inside the first one.

SUMMARY

In the first three chapters of this book, you have found out how to set up your computer and how to use it with commercial software packages. You then learned to give the computer a command of your own, which made it PRINT a message on the screen.

In this chapter, you have learned the essentials of your computer's graphics system. You used coordinates in the POSITION statement to place text messages where you wanted them on the screen. Then, you learned to display points and lines in the four-color graphics mode. All of these commands will be useful to you in the pages ahead.

The main thing you lack now is a way to save your commands. The procedure for drawing a box, for instance, took seven separate commands, each of which had to be entered from the keyboard. Suppose you wanted to draw the box again. You would have to go through those seven steps all over again.

There is an easier way, and that is the subject of Section Two.

Section 2

Programming

CHAPTER FIVE

Writing a Program

In Section One of this book, you have seen some of the things you can do with your computer. You have learned how to give commands that print messages and draw simple pictures. As you gave your commands, the computer immediately put them into action.

There has been one great limitation, however. You have had to type every command in from the keyboard. If you made a small mistake in a series of commands, you have had to clear the screen and start over from the beginning. Also, if you wanted to repeat a certain task (such as drawing a box), you have had to retype the whole series of commands every time. Because of this, you have been limited to very short procedures.

With a *program,* you can store a series of commands in the computer's memory, then run them all as a group. When so instructed, the computer reacts to the commands as if you had just typed them in from the keyboard. And when the computer has finished, the commands are still stored, ready to be reused. If one of the steps was wrong, or if you want to try a variation, you are free to alter the program and run it again.

Because programs let you design a procedure and reuse it many times, they make it practical to do more complicated tasks on your computer. If you were restricted to typing your commands one by one, you would never want to try anything much more complex than

```
PRINT "HELLO"
```

With stored programs, you can easily combine many commands into powerful procedures that you can use over and over. Many people create programs involving hundreds of stored commands.

As you will discover in future chapters, programs also give you new kinds of control over what your computer is doing. In a program, you can store words and numbers as you go along, and perform calculations. You can take a group of commands and run them over and over in a loop, or have your computer do something only if a certain condition is fulfilled. With these tools, you will be able to direct your computer to perform complex tasks, then sit back while it does the work.

This chapter will show you how to store a program in the computer's memory and how to run it. It will give a few short examples to get you started.

In learning to write programs, you will be mastering a *programming language.* Computer designers long ago realized that their machines were too literal to understand complex English sentences, which are often full of ambiguity. Instead, they decided to make up a system of commands which are easy to learn yet specific enough for the computer to understand.

With your Atari computer, you will be using Atari's version of a language called BASIC. This stands for "Beginners' All-purpose Symbolic Instruction Code"—if you can believe that. As its name implies, BASIC is easy to learn and simple to use; because of this, it has become the most popular language for small computers such as the Atari 600XL and 800XL. You have already been using some commands from the Atari BASIC language (including PRINT, GRAPHICS, and COLOR). You will now be able to use these and other commands in the programs that you write.

Let's see how it's done.

STORING YOUR PROGRAM

Your program consists of a series of commands, stored in the computer's memory. When you are ready to use the stored commands, you tell the computer to RUN the program. It then carries them out one after the other.

Before you do anything else, press RESET on your computer and type the word

```
NEW
```

When you press the RETURN key, the computer will clear everything from its memory and give you a clean slate to type your program.

You should give this NEW command every time you begin a new program, even when you have RESET the machine. If you don't, there may be program lines left in the computer's memory from some other task. If you leave these lines in the memory, they may slip into the program you are typing and disrupt it. You should make the NEW command a habit.

You can store any Atari command as a line in a program, just by placing a number in front of it. This is called a *statement number,* and it serves as a signal that you want the computer to store the command rather than to put it into immediate action.

Back in Chapter 3, you typed your first command from the keyboard:

```
PRINT "HELLO"
```

When you pressed RETURN, the computer immediately did as it was told, and displayed the word HELLO on the screen. Now let's try a small variation. Type the following line:

```
10 PRINT "HELLO"
```

When you press RETURN, nothing seems to happen. The number 10 before the word PRINT told the computer just to store the line in its memory. There is nothing special about the number 10; we could have used any number.

You can check to see that the line is stored by typing another command:

```
LIST
```

This tells the computer to display all of the lines it has in its memory. In this case, there is only line number 10.

Now let's ask the computer to carry out the stored command. To do this, type the word

```
RUN
```

and press RETURN. You get the same result as you did when you typed the command without a number: the computer prints the word HELLO on the screen. The action is delayed, however, until you give the RUN command.

If you type RUN a second time, the computer will repeat the word HELLO. You can do this as many times as you like: your command remains stored in the computer's memory until you turn the power off or type NEW to clear the memory.

To add a second line to your program, just type another command with a different number in front of it. Again, this could be any number, but since we used 10 as our statement number for our first command, let's use 20 for the second:

```
20 PRINT "HELLO AGAIN"
```

When you press RETURN, the second statement will be stored in the memory along with the first.

You can see how your program now looks by typing LIST. Your computer will respond by typing all of the statements it has stored:

```
10 PRINT "HELLO"
20 PRINT "HELLO AGAIN"
```

Each statement is stored as a unit. The computer keeps them in the order determined by the statement numbers, regardless of the order in which you typed them.

You now have two program lines in the computer's memory. What will happen when you type RUN? The computer will search through its memory and follow the stored commands in sequence. After it has finished, it will drop down and say READY once again. The result will look like this:

```
HELLO
HELLO AGAIN

READY
```

You can add statements anywhere you want to in your program. Suppose we wanted a message between the two lines. All we have to do is type a command with a statement number between 10 and 20, and it will be filed in the proper place. We might, for example, choose the number 15:

```
15 PRINT "GOODBYE"
```

If you LIST the program, you can see that the new statement has taken its place between the other two:

```
10  PRINT "HELLO"
15  PRINT "GOODBYE"
20  PRINT "HELLO AGAIN"
```

RUN the program. The new command will be carried out in the order of its statement number:

```
HELLO
GOODBYE
HELLO AGAIN

READY
```

You can choose any number from 0 to 32767 for your statement numbers. You would do best, however, to use multiples of ten (10, 20, 30, etc.). This gives an ordered appearance to your program, and leaves plenty of room for insertions.

To delete a line, just type the statement number followed by nothing. Suppose you want to eliminate the last line, HELLO AGAIN. Just type

```
20
```

and press RETURN. The statement numbered 20 will now be erased from the computer's memory, as you can tell by LISTing the program once again:

```
10  PRINT "HELLO"
15  PRINT "GOODBYE"
```

If you now RUN the program, the computer will use only the statements that remain:

```
HELLO
GOODBYE

READY
```

If you want to change a line, type a new version using the same statement number:

```
10  PRINT "HELLO THERE"
```

When you press RETURN, this line will replace the old version of statement number 10. Your program will now look like this:

```
10 PRINT "HELLO THERE"
15 PRINT "GOODBYE"
```

It is important to remember that you can use each statement number only once. If you duplicate a number, your new statement will replace the previous one.

If you only want to make a minor change in a program line, you can use the editing functions you learned in Chapter 3. As you may recall, you can change any command that you can see on the screen. You merely move the cursor to it, make your correction, and press RETURN to enter the new version into the computer's memory.

You can only edit statements that are displayed on the screen. What if you want to change a line that is not currently displayed? You could LIST the whole program again, but it is simpler to display just the line you want to change. You can LIST a particular line with a command like this:

```
LIST 15
```

Only line 15 will be displayed:

```
15 PRINT "GOODBYE"
```

Suppose you want to insert an exclamation after GOODBYE. Move the cursor until it is covering the second quotation mark, as shown in Figure 5.1. Now press CONTROL and the INSERT key to open up a space in the line between the word GOODBYE and the quotation mark. Then type an exclamation point, and you will have the line the way you want it. (Review Chapter 3 if you are confused by these editing commands.)

You have corrected the line, but it is not yet stored in the computer's memory. To store it, press the RETURN key: the corrected line will replace the previous version and become part of the program. As far as the computer is concerned, you do the same thing by editing a line as you would by typing it in from the beginning. The computer doesn't care whether you retyped the entire line or simply changed a character in a line that it had LISTed. No matter how the line got on the screen, the computer takes it and stores it as part of the program.

Use LIST to make sure your change has been incorporated:

```
10  PRINT "HELLO THERE"
15  PRINT "GOODBYE!"
```

Sometimes you will want to type a command such as RUN or LIST when your cursor is not on a blank line. You can ask the computer to give you a blank line by pressing the SHIFT and INSERT keys together. You can also type CONTROL-CLEAR, if you don't mind erasing the entire screen.

As a review, let's go back over the different ways you can use statement numbers as you type your program.

- *Add* If you enter a line with a statement number that you haven't used before, it will be stored as a new line of your program.
- *Insert* If you type a line with a statement number between two other numbers already stored, the line will be inserted in the program at that point.

Figure 5.1: *Editing a program line.*

- *Replace* If you enter a line with a statement number that has already been used, your new version will replace the old.
- *Delete* If you enter a statement number with no command following, the computer will delete any statement stored under that number.

You now know everything you'll need to type programs into the computer. You know how to add, insert, replace, and delete program lines. You know how to LIST your program, and how to run it.

It is time for a practical example.

THE BOX-DRAWING PROGRAM

At the end of Chapter 4, you typed a sequence of seven graphics commands to draw a box on the screen. To review, try the same series again:

```
GRAPHICS 7
COLOR 1
PLOT 10,10
DRAWTO 70,10
DRAWTO 70,70
DRAWTO 10,70
DRAWTO 10,10
```

The computer will shift into the four-color graphics mode and produce a picture that resembles Figure 4.6 on page 58.

We're going to be writing a new program, so press RESET to return to the text mode and type the command

```
NEW
```

to clear the computer's memory. Remember: a program line remains in the memory until you either delete it, clean the slate with a NEW command, or turn the computer off.

What we're going to do now is simple. We're going to retype the seven commands, but this time we'll give them numbers and store them as a program. Type these lines:

```
10 GRAPHICS 7
20 COLOR 1
30 PLOT 10,10
```

```
40  DRAWTO 70,10
50  DRAWTO 70,70
60  DRAWTO 10,70
70  DRAWTO 10,10
```

When you're done, check your typing to make sure you haven't made any mistakes. If necessary, retype the line, or correct it with your editing keys.

Now RUN the program. Almost instantly, your computer will shift to the black graphics screen and draw an orange box. The result is the same as Figure 4.6, but the computer did it all in one step, rather than seven.

With a procedure as long as this, the advantages of stored programs become evident. You can correct a mistake by editing, rather than going back to the beginning. You can draw the box again with a single RUN command, rather than retyping all seven steps. As we go on, you will discover other advantages to writing programs, and other uses to which they can be put.

HINTS ON WRITING PROGRAMS

As you write your own programs, you will need to develop some habits that make your work easier. Clear thinking and good organization are often the difference between successful programming and computer nightmares. Here are three rules to follow:

1. *Think it through.* You will save yourself a lot of agony if you spend a few minutes planning out your program before you start typing it. You don't have to write the program out in full unless you feel the need, but you should sketch out the route before you embark on your journey.

2. *Be neat.* There is nothing more frustrating than trying to make corrections in a sloppy program. If you organize your program so that it is easy to read and logical in its layout, you will understand it much better when you go back to change it. Use a regular pattern in your statement numbers, such as 10, 20, 30.

3. *Leave notes to yourself.* Your computer lets you leave comments in the middle of your program. Comments that explain what you are trying to do will make your program much easier to understand.

To leave a note at a certain point in your program, type an unused statement number and the letters REM (for "remark"). You can then type anything you choose on the rest of the line. For example, at the beginning of the box-drawing program you might want to add a line that announces its purpose. Try the following:

```
5  REM PROGRAM TO DRAW A BOX
```

When you LIST the program, this remark will appear at the head. When you RUN the program, however, the computer will ignore the remark.

You may feel these remarks are a waste of time, if you are only writing programs for yourself: you know what you're doing, and the computer doesn't need the explanations. Don't kid yourself. Even if you understand the program perfectly now, you won't remember it six months from now if you decide to revise it. Also, if you give your program to a friend, you will want to include enough information to explain what you have done.

Figure 5.2 shows how remarks can be used to explain the box-drawing program. Asterisks were placed around the title of the program to set it apart. Blank REM statements in lines 8, 24, and 34 are used to separate the program into its major parts. The REM statements 9, 25, and 35 name the parts. By judiciously using remarks in this way, you can make the structure of your program much more visible.

DEBUGGING

No matter how careful you are in writing your programs, you will certainly have troubles from time to time. Your program doesn't work exactly the way you want it to, or you get an ERROR when you try to RUN it. This is known as a *bug* in your program, and you are faced with the task of *debugging*.

The first thing to check is the ERROR message, if there was one. If, for example, your screen looks like Figure 5.3 when you try to RUN the box-drawing program, you have a pretty good idea where to look. The computer was partway through the program, then something went wrong when it reached statement 60.

What does this ERROR message mean?

```
ERROR-- 3 AT LINE 60
```

The 3 in this message is a code that describes what the problem was. To translate it into English, look the code up in Appendix C of this book. You will find that 3 means "Value Error." This is one of the most common errors on the Atari computer, and it usually comes from typing an incorrect number, or a number too large for the place where it's being used. This is the ERROR you get if you try to PLOT or DRAWTO a point with a coordinate that is too large for the graphics screen.

Once you know where the error occurred, LIST the program and check it over. In this case, line 60 is the most likely place for the error, but you should look at the other statements as well. Often a mistake in an earlier line will cause problems in a perfectly good line later on.

Check the program over, line by line. Pay particular attention to details; a missing comma or a misspelled word can block an entire program.

Check to make sure that no lines are missing. It is easy to leave out a command as you are typing, or to erase one by typing the wrong

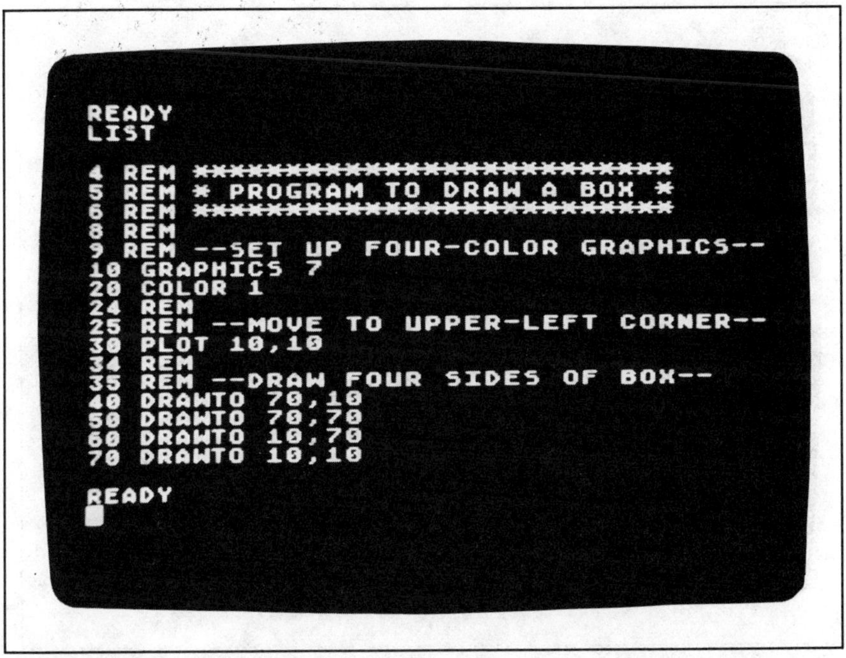

```
READY
LIST

4 REM ****************************
5 REM * PROGRAM TO DRAW A BOX *
6 REM ****************************
8 REM
9 REM --SET UP FOUR-COLOR GRAPHICS--
10 GRAPHICS 7
20 COLOR 1
24 REM
25 REM --MOVE TO UPPER-LEFT CORNER--
30 PLOT 10,10
34 REM
35 REM --DRAW FOUR SIDES OF BOX--
40 DRAWTO 70,10
50 DRAWTO 70,70
60 DRAWTO 10,70
70 DRAWTO 10,10

READY
```

Figure 5.2: *Use REM statements in your programs to make them more readable.*

statement number. Make sure also that no unwanted lines have slipped into your program. For example, you might have forgotten to give a NEW command before you started typing.

If you still can't find your mistake, have a friend check your program over. Often another person will be able to spot a small mistake that you had missed. Try explaining your program to someone else. This will frequently uncover a gap in your reasoning.

After you have exhausted all the other alternatives, you may be tempted to think it is the computer's fault. This is unlikely. Computers are very reliable in following their instructions, and they are rarely at fault for the errors. Usually, it is a breakdown in the communication between you and the machine: what you thought you were writing is not what the computer took you to mean.

You should suspect the computer itself only if it starts behaving erratically on a variety of programs, or on programs which you've already tested out. If your machine is defective, the problems will usually be obvious, and will affect the computer's overall functioning,

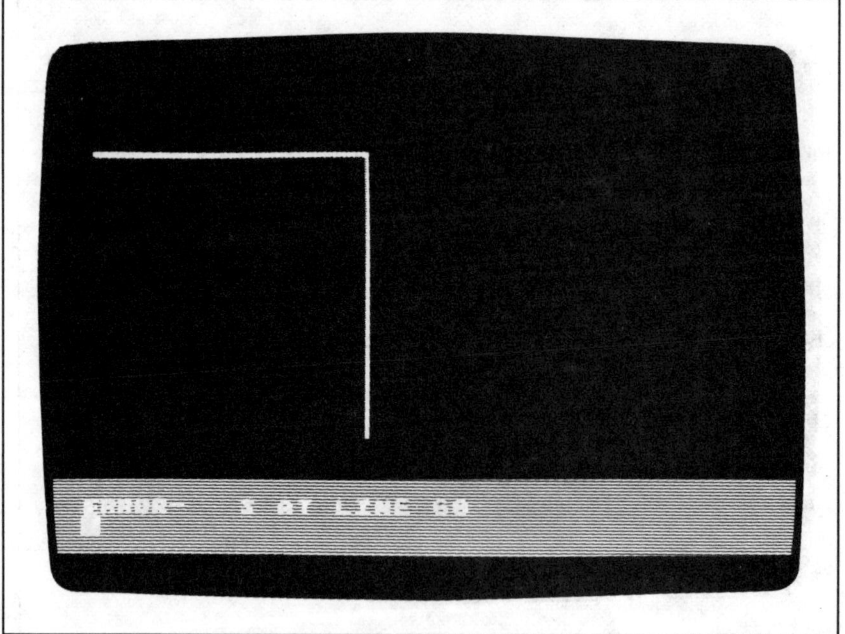

Figure 5.3: *A typical ERROR message.*

rather than just a single program. Check with your dealer if you feel that your machine has gone bad.

Have courage. It can be very difficult to debug a program, so don't become frustrated. Often when you do find the bug, it will seem like a silly mistake. But don't blame yourself for having overlooked the error. It happens to everyone.

CASSETTE STORAGE

You can store only one program at a time in your computer's memory. If you wish to use a different program, you must erase the first one by typing NEW. Your program is also lost when you turn the power off.

This is a problem if you have written a program that you want to use over and over. Unless you can leave the computer on indefinitely and use it only for that one program, you will need to retype the program every time you want to run it.

If you have an Atari Program Recorder or Disk Drive, you can save your programs permanently and load them back into the computer's memory whenever you want to use them. This is very handy—well worth the investment if you plan to write long programs.

At this point in the book, I will not take the time to tell you exactly how to use the program recorder or the disk drive. Instead, I have collected all of the detailed instructions in Chapters 9 and 10. If you want to learn about your cassette recorder or disk drive right now, skip ahead to these chapters: you can read them without knowing the material in Chapters 6 through 8.

Just for convenience, however, I will explain the simplest of these operations: saving a program on cassette tape and loading it back in. If you get hung up on these directions, or if you are using a disk drive rather than a cassette recorder, you should read the detailed instructions in Chapters 9 and 10.

Start by connecting your Atari Program Recorder. You can use either the new model 1010 or the old model 410; both will work with any Atari computer. You must plug the recorder into a wall outlet, then connect its special black cable to the large hole on the back of your computer labeled PERIPHERAL. Refer to Chapter 9 if you don't know how to do this.

You can now save the program in the computer's memory on a

regular cassette tape. Any tape will do, even the cheapest. Put the tape in the recorder and rewind it to the beginning. Then type the following command:

```
CSAVE
```

This tells the computer that you want it to save the program on the cassette. When you press RETURN, the computer will beep twice through your television as a cue for you to record. Press PLAY and RECORD on the program recorder. Press RETURN again.

Your computer will start to whistle: this is the actual sound it is recording on the tape. It means nothing to you, but to the computer it contains all of the information needed for your program. The recording process takes about 20 seconds (more if your program is very long). The recorder will stop automatically when it is finished, and the computer will say READY. With your program on tape, you can safely erase it from the computer's memory or turn the computer off.

To load the program back into the memory you must use a similar procedure. Type

```
CLOAD
```

and press RETURN. The computer will beep once, asking you to start the recorder. Rewind the tape and press the PLAY button. Press RETURN again. The recorder will turn and the computer will load the program. When it has finished, the recorder will stop and the computer will say READY. You can now LIST the program to make sure it was loaded correctly, then you can RUN it again. Note that the program you load will replace any program you had previously stored in the computer's memory.

If you have any problems with these brief directions, please read Chapter 9. The descriptions there are much more complete, and contain other helpful suggestions. This is just to get you started.

OPTIONAL EXERCISES

1. In the box-drawing program on pages 70-71, add a statement that will make the last line in the box blue. You will have to choose a statement number between 60 and 70.
2. Add a line at the end of the same program, to draw a

diagonal line from the upper-left corner of the square to the lower right.

3. The following program contains three mistakes:

```
10 PRINT "HELLO THERE"
20 GRAPHICS 7
30 COLOR 1
40 PLOT 10,734
50 DRAWTO 0,0
60 DRAWTO 10
```

Find the bugs.

SUMMARY

In this chapter, you have seen how you can string your commands together to make a program. You can store as many commands as you like in the computer's memory, and RUN them all as a group. You can use the LIST command to review the program you have stored, or to make changes in it.

Programs have many uses, as you have already seen. Since they can be changed and reused as often as you like, programs allow you to try much more complicated operations than you would if you needed to type the commands each time. If you have a cassette recorder, you can even save the program permanently for future use.

In the next two chapters of this book, you will learn techniques that make this concept much more flexible. You will increase your control over your computer and discover its true power.

CHAPTER SIX

Using Variables

So far, you have been giving very specific instructions to your computer. You have told it to PRINT a word or to PLOT a point at a given coordinate. If you want to PRINT a different word or PLOT a different point, however, you have to type a whole new command.

You can make your commands much more flexible if you are less specific. Your computer allows you to replace numbers with *variables,* labels which can stand for any number you choose. As you RUN the program, you specify what numbers the variables will represent. Later you can run the program with the variables standing for different numbers.

Variables also let you use your computer for calculations. Your computer can do arithmetic quickly and accurately, then display the results on the screen. This can save you many hours of work. At the end of this chapter, you will learn how you can make variables represent letters as well as numbers, so that you can manipulate words as well.

In this chapter, we will try out several variations on the program that draws a box on the screen. The idea remains the same as the program we developed in Chapter 5; this time, however, we will use variables to stand for the coordinates. This will make it much easier to change the shape and location of the box the program draws.

STORING NUMBERS

Computers generally prefer to do their thinking with numbers, rather than words. In most of our commands, we have used one or more numbers to tell the computer what we wanted. To PLOT a point, for instance, we used a pair of numbers to name its coordinates.

To use a fixed number such as 46, you just type its digits. In general, you can type the number exactly as you would normally write it. When it is greater than 1,000, however, you should leave out the comma that separates the thousands from the hundreds.

These are all *fixed numbers*. You can type a fixed number in any command, but it is used immediately rather than stored. If you want to reuse the number, you will have to type it out again.

There is a way, however, to store a number in your computer, so that you can reuse it without retyping it. To do this, you give the number a name. You can call it anything you want, just as long as you begin the name with a letter.

You might, for example, want to call it FRED. To store the number 7, all you need to do is type

```
FRED=7
```

When you press RETURN, your computer sets aside a place in its memory for the variable FRED. It then stores the number 7 in that place, so that you can refer to it by name.

You cannot turn this equation around, as you can in normal arithmetic. If you type

```
7=FRED
```

you are saying, "Take the number FRED and store it under the name 7." This makes no sense to the computer, and you will get an ERROR.

The computer actually thinks of the equal sign as a command. When it sees this sign, it looks for whatever value is to the *right* of the sign, then stores that value in the name to the left. This is called an *assignment statement.*

The name FRED now represents the number 7. You can see this by asking the computer to PRINT the value:

```
PRINT FRED
```

If you do this, the computer will display the number 7. (If it displays 0 or something else, you have probably mistyped something: try typing the last two commands again.)

You can now use the name FRED anywhere you would normally use the number 7. You could switch into the four-color graphics mode by typing

```
GRAPHICS FRED
```

You could PLOT the point 7,7 by typing

```
PLOT FRED,FRED
```

You could even store the number 7 in another variable named JANE by setting it equal to FRED:

```
JANE=FRED
```

Let's look a little more carefully at the statement

```
PRINT FRED
```

When you pressed RETURN, the computer displayed the value you had given to the name FRED. Notice that the result is very different from what you would get if you said

```
PRINT "FRED"
```

If you do this, the computer will type the word FRED on the screen, rather than its value. With the quotes, the computer reads "FRED" as a message to be displayed. Without the quotes, it reads FRED as the name for the stored number, and displays its value.

The stored number is called a *variable,* because you can change its value. To do this, you merely store a new value. The computer will accept it, and replace the old value with it.

To change FRED's value to 19, type

```
FRED=19
```

The old value (7) will be lost, and FRED will mean 19 from now on. You can check this by giving the command

```
PRINT FRED
```

FRED will continue to mean 19 until you store another value or turn the computer off.

Until you use a variable, the computer assumes its value is 0. You can see this by printing a name you haven't used:

```
PRINT IRVING
```

The computer will respond with the number 0, since you haven't given a value to the variable IRVING.

So far, we have been using people's names, like FRED, JANE, and IRVING. It is generally best, however, to use a word that explains what the variable represents. If you have a variable that counts the number of times you have done an operation, you might call it COUNTER. For graphics, you might want to call the coordinates of a point X and Y, so that you can simply say

```
PLOT X,Y
```

When you are plotting more than one point, you might give your coordinates different names all starting with X and Y. For example, if you were drawing a line from one point to another, you might call the starting point XSTART, YSTART and the ending point XEND, YEND.

There are only a few restrictions on the names you can choose for your variables. The name can be as long as you wish, but it must begin with a letter. The rest of the name can contain numbers, but no special symbols. You may not use lowercase letters or inverse video in your variable names. Finally, you may not start your variable name with an Atari command word, such as PRINT or PLOT. The computer would have no way to tell the difference between your variable and the command.

Within these guidelines, you can use any name you like. The names in the left column of Figure 6.1 show some of the possibilities. The right column shows some examples of illegal words. You don't need to be too concerned, though, since most of the names you would use are legal.

In these experiments with stored values, you have seen how variables work. You can store a number in any variable you choose, then use the variable's name instead of the number. If you want to change the number, you merely store a new value. The variable will represent the new value until you change it again.

LEGAL	ILLEGAL	(REASON)
DATE	123	Doesn't begin with a letter
NUMBER	BILL'SBILLS	Contains a special symbol
SIDE4	Wilhelm	Not capital letters
DELAY	THE NUMBER	More than one word
N	GRAPHICS	Atari command word

Figure 6.1: *Legal and illegal variable names.*

VARIABLES IN PROGRAMS

When you're just typing simple commands, variables don't seem all that useful. As long as you are typing each command as you go, you might as well use the fixed number instead.

In programs, however, variables become very important. With them, you can write a general procedure that accomplishes a certain task, without knowing what specific numbers you will be using on any particular occasion. When you RUN the program, you can plug in the specific numbers you want. If you later want to perform the same task with different numbers, you simply RUN the program again with the new values.

To see how this works, let's return to the program to draw a box that we developed in Chapters 4 and 5. To start off, give a NEW command and type the program back into the computer's memory, as follows:

```
4 REM ******************
5 REM * PROGRAM TO DRAW A BOX *
6 REM ******************
8 REM
9 REM -SET UP FOUR-COLOR GRAPHICS-
10 GRAPHICS 7
20 COLOR 1
100 REM
101 REM -MOVE TO UPPER-LEFT CORNER-
110 PLOT 10,10
120 REM
121 REM -DRAW FOUR SIDES OF BOX-
130 DRAWTO 70,10
140 DRAWTO 70,70
150 DRAWTO 10,70
160 DRAWTO 10,10
```

This program is exactly the same as the one shown in Figure 5.2, except that the statement numbers have been changed in the second half. This was done to make room, because we're going to add some statements between numbers 20 and 100. If you want to save yourself some typing, you can skip some of the REM statements, which do not affect the operation of the program.

In every version of this program that we have used, our box has always been the same size, and it has always been in the same location. The coordinates we used to set the corners are fixed numbers. The box starts at the coordinates 10,10—a point near the upper-left corner of the screen. Each edge is then drawn to a fixed point, until the final edge returns to the starting point. Figure 6.2 shows the fixed coordinates of each corner of the box.

We can make our program more general so that it can draw a box of any size, shape, or location. Instead of using fixed coordinates for the corners, we can use variables.

Figure 6.3 shows the names we'll be using for each of the points. These names were chosen to explain the numbers they will represent. XLEFT, for example, gives the x-coordinate of the left side of the box. Note that each of the variables is used in the names of two different corners: XLEFT is the x-coordinate of both the upper-left and lower-left corners.

Let's begin changing the program from numbers to variables. Instead of giving another NEW command and retyping everything, just type the new lines that you want to add. As you may recall, when you type an additional line while you have a program stored in the memory, the new line will be inserted into the program. If its statement number matches one already in the program, the old statement

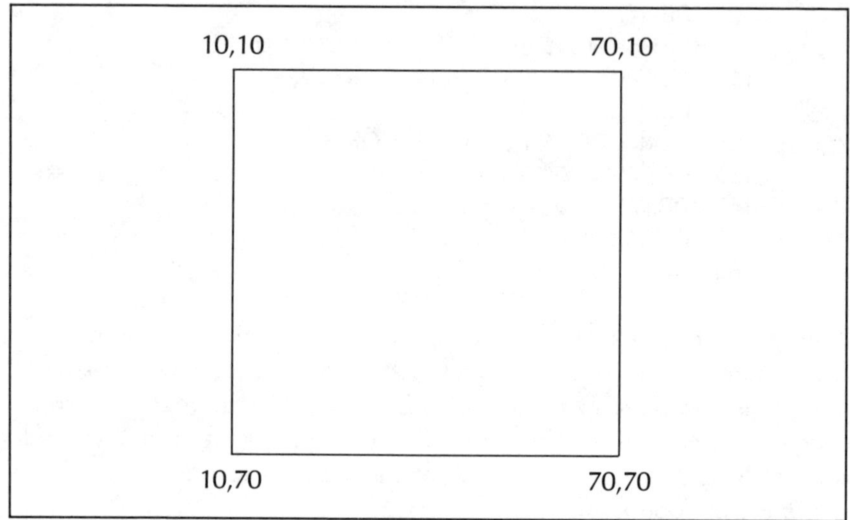

Figure 6.2: *With fixed numbers, you can only have a square of one size.*

will be replaced. In this way we will be able to change certain parts of the program without retyping the whole thing.

There are times in this chapter when you will RUN a program that will leave the screen in the graphics mode. You can type commands in the text window at the bottom of the screen, but you will usually find it easier to return to the text mode. You can do this either by typing GRAPHICS 0, or by pressing RESET.

Before we can use the four variables to name the corners of the box, we need to store their values. We could choose any numbers we want, but let's start with the coordinates we've been using: 10 and 70. Insert the following five lines into your program:

```
30  REM -STORE VALUES IN VARIABLES-
40  XLEFT=10
50  XRIGHT=70
60  YTOP=10
70  YBOTTOM=70
```

Now that we have the values stored, we can retype the PLOT and DRAWTO statements using the variables instead of fixed numbers. Type five lines as follows:

```
110  PLOT XLEFT,YTOP
130  DRAWTO XRIGHT,YTOP
```

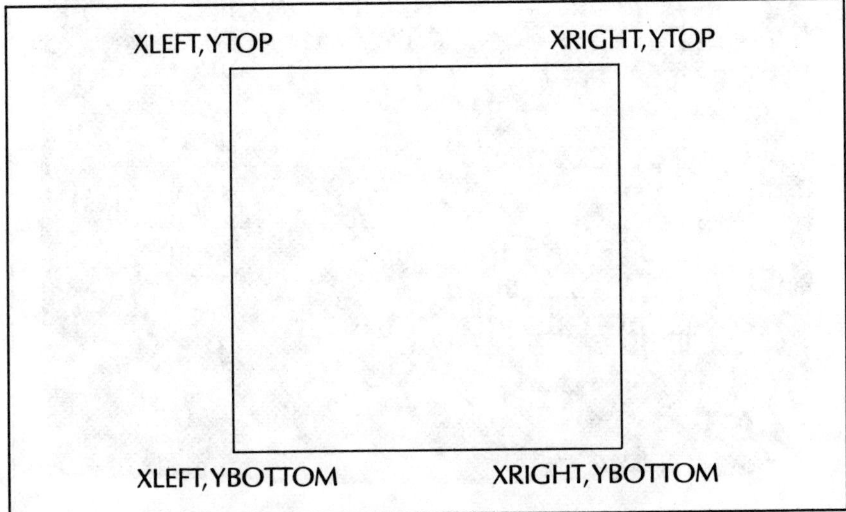

Figure 6.3: *We will give these variable names to the corners of the box.*

```
140 DRAWTO XRIGHT,YBOTTOM
150 DRAWTO XLEFT,YBOTTOM
160 DRAWTO XLEFT,YTOP
```

These lines will replace the PLOT and DRAWTO statements in the original program.

LIST the program to make sure that all of your new statements have been stored correctly. Check the lines you have just added, to make sure they are accurate. The program should exactly match the listing shown in Figure 6.4.

When you're sure you have it right, RUN the program. You should get exactly the same results as you did with the original version: an orange box on the left half of the screen. This is because the variables used in the PLOT and DRAWTO statements contained exactly the same values (10 and 70) as the fixed coordinates did in the original version.

With the variable version, however, you can change the shape of

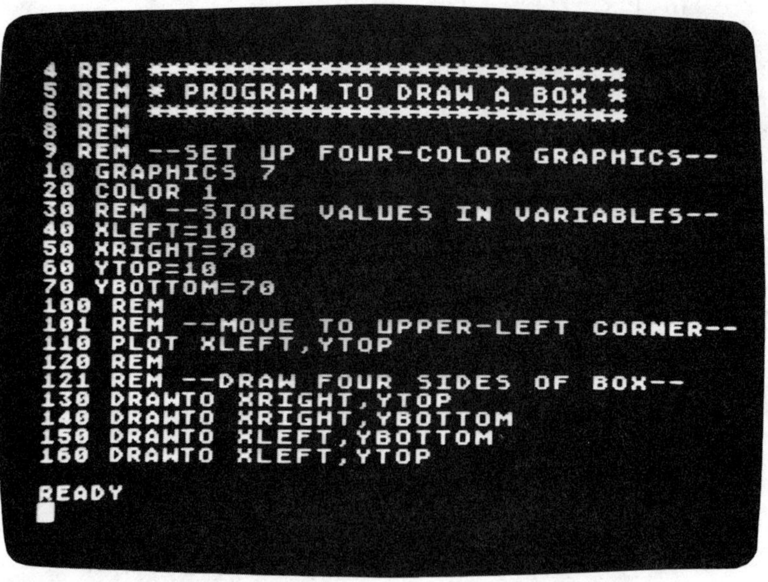

```
4 REM ***************************
5 REM * PROGRAM TO DRAW A BOX *
6 REM ***************************
8 REM
9 REM --SET UP FOUR-COLOR GRAPHICS--
10 GRAPHICS 7
20 COLOR 1
30 REM --STORE VALUES IN VARIABLES--
40 XLEFT=10
50 XRIGHT=70
60 YTOP=10
70 YBOTTOM=70
100 REM
101 REM --MOVE TO UPPER-LEFT CORNER--
110 PLOT XLEFT,YTOP
120 REM
121 REM --DRAW FOUR SIDES OF BOX--
130 DRAWTO XRIGHT,YTOP
140 DRAWTO XRIGHT,YBOTTOM
150 DRAWTO XLEFT,YBOTTOM
160 DRAWTO XLEFT,YTOP

READY
```

Figure 6.4: *The revised version of the box-drawing program.*

the box by modifying the statements that store the values. Replace statements 40 through 70 with the following:

```
40  XLEFT=20
50  XRIGHT=140
60  YTOP=35
70  YBOTTOM=45
```

If you LIST the program, you will see that the new statements 40 through 70 have replaced the old. When you RUN the program, these new values produce a thin horizontal rectangle across the screen, as shown in Figure 6.5. By choosing other values for these four variables, you can produce rectangles of any dimensions. Type and RUN these two other combinations:

```
40  XLEFT=75          40 XLEFT=0
50  XRIGHT=85         50 XRIGHT=159
60  YTOP=10           60 YTOP=0
70  YBOTTOM=70        70 YBOTTOM=79
```

Figure 6.5: *Using variables, you can draw a box of any size.*

With the example at the left, you will get a thin vertical box. With the values at the right, the computer will draw a yellow rectangle around the entire graphics screen.

Try out some values of your own in this program. You can change any of the variables you want, then RUN the program. The computer will draw a box according to the dimensions you give. You can choose any numbers you want for the variables, as long as you don't exceed the limits on the X and Y dimensions of the graphics screen. X must fall between 0 and 159, and Y between 0 and 79, or you will get an ERROR.

Notice that the variable XLEFT occurs three times in the PLOT and DRAWTO lines of the program, yet you can use one new assignment statement to change its value in all three places. No matter how many times a variable occurs in a program, one new assignment will change its value throughout.

By using variables, we have made a real improvement over the earlier versions of this box-drawing program. We can now tell the computer exactly where to put the four edges of the box and how large to make it. More important, we were able to design the program to perform a general task, then change specific numbers without rewriting the entire program.

*THE **READ** AND **DATA** STATEMENTS*

When you have wanted to change the value of a variable you are using in a program, you have needed to go back and change the statement where you stored it. This is all right if you rarely make changes, or if they only involve one variable. If, however, you frequently need to change many values in a program, there is a better way: your computer lets you assign values to several variables in a single statement. You do this with two new commands: READ and DATA.

READ and DATA always work as a pair, and you cannot use one without the other. In the READ statement, you give the computer a list of variables to which you wish to assign values. You then type a DATA statement with a corresponding list of the numbers that you want to store. The computer takes the first value from the list in the DATA statement and assigns it to the first variable in the READ statement. If there are more variables to be filled, it returns to the DATA statement and stores the second value in the second variable in the READ statement. This process continues until all of the variables have been filled. You must have at least enough values in the DATA statement to fill all of the variables. If you run out of numbers to read, you will get an error.

To see how this works, let's revise lines 30 through 70 of the box-writing program to use READ and DATA statements. Type the following lines:

```
30 REM -READ VALUES INTO VARIABLES-
40 READ XLEFT,XRIGHT,YTOP,YBOTTOM
50 DATA 10,70,10,70
```

When you're done typing this, add two more blank lines, to delete unwanted statements left over from the previous version:

```
60
70
```

LIST the program: it should match Figure 6.6. When you RUN the program, you will get the same results as before—a large yellow box on the left half of the screen.

The four variables in the READ statement correspond exactly to the four values in the DATA. When the computer comes to the READ statement, it plugs the first number from the DATA statement (10) into the first variable (XLEFT). It then continues, with the other variables, reading 70 into XRIGHT, 10 into YTOP, and 70 into YBOTTOM. These two lines have the same effect as the four lines we replaced:

```
40 XLEFT=10
50 XRIGHT=70
60 YTOP=10
70 YBOTTOM=70
```

The READ and DATA statements, however, are easier to type and to understand.

The great advantage of READ and DATA statements is that you can easily change to new values. If you want to draw a thin horizontal box, as in Figure 6.5, you need to type only a new DATA statement:

```
50 DATA 20,140,35,45
```

When the computer draws the box, the corners are set by the new values.

You can experiment with many different numbers in this DATA statement. In the previous version, you had to replace four lines, but here you need to retype only the one DATA statement. Try these sets of values:

```
50 DATA 75,85,10,70
```

and

```
50 DATA 0,159,0,79
```

You should get yellow rectangles of other shapes, just as you did on page 87. Try some other values of your own.

INPUT: GETTING VALUES FROM THE KEYBOARD

There is a third way to assign numbers to variables, which is even more flexible than the READ statement. This is the INPUT statement, which has the computer pause in the middle of the program

```
LIST

4 REM ***************************
5 REM * PROGRAM TO DRAW A BOX *
6 REM ***************************
8 REM
9 REM --SET UP FOUR-COLOR GRAPHICS--
10 GRAPHICS 7
20 COLOR 1
30 REM --READ VALUES INTO VARIABLES--
40 READ XLEFT,XRIGHT,YTOP,YBOTTOM
50 DATA 10,70,10,70
100 REM
101 REM --MOVE TO UPPER-LEFT CORNER--
110 PLOT XLEFT,YTOP
120 REM
121 REM --DRAW FOUR SIDES OF BOX--
130 DRAWTO XRIGHT,YTOP
140 DRAWTO XRIGHT,YBOTTOM
150 DRAWTO XLEFT,YBOTTOM
160 DRAWTO XLEFT,YTOP

READY
```

Figure 6.6: *The box-drawing program, using READ and DATA statements.*

and ask you to type in a value on the keyboard. With this, you will no longer need to specify the numbers as you are writing the program. Instead, you can supply the values at the time you RUN the program. This also means that you can RUN the same program with different values merely by giving different responses.

To have the computer ask you for the value of the first variable, XLEFT, you could put this line into the box-writing program:

```
40  INPUT XLEFT
```

When you ask the computer to RUN the program, it will stop when it comes to this statement and put a question mark on the screen. This is a *prompt* to show that the computer is waiting for you to supply some information.

Most people use a PRINT statement just before the INPUT statement, so that they can know which piece of information the computer is waiting for. I'd suggest you use something like this:

```
40  PRINT "LEFT EDGE";:INPUT XLEFT
```

If you RUN a program with this statement, the computer will pause and type the following message:

```
LEFT EDGE?
```

This tells you which value the computer is expecting you to supply.

Notice the two punctuation marks (;:) before the word INPUT in this line. You learned the meaning of the colon (:) back in Chapter 3: it separates two statements written on the same line of a program. The semicolon (;) serves a different purpose. When you type a semicolon at the end of a PRINT statement, it keeps the computer from starting a new line at the end of its message. After the end of the message, the INPUT statement automatically types a question mark. The result will be a very readable question.

To see the INPUT statement in action, let's make yet another revision of our box-drawing program. Type the following lines:

```
30  REM  -GET VALUES FROM KEYBOARD-
40  PRINT "LEFT EDGE";:INPUT XLEFT
50  PRINT "RIGHT EDGE";:INPUT XRIGHT
60  PRINT "TOP";:INPUT YTOP
70  PRINT "BOTTOM";:INPUT YBOTTOM
```

If you LIST the new version of the program, it should look like Figure 6.7. Note that the variables in this program are never given explicit values.

When you RUN this program, it will work a little differently from the other versions. The computer first shifts into the four-color graphics mode, following the instructions in lines 10 and 20. Then, at statement number 40, it prints the message LEFT EDGE? in the text window and stops. This is your cue to type the first number—the coordinate of the left edge of the box (XLEFT). The computer will wait until you type a number and press RETURN. After you do that, it will ask for three more numbers to set the coordinates of the other three edges of the box. You might give the answers shown in Figure 6.8.

When you're typing in your values as you RUN the program, you can use the keyboard just as you do normally. You can correct mistakes with the BACK SPACE key, and you can type as many digits as you wish. Once you press the RETURN key, however, the computer stores your answer in its memory, and you cannot go back. Of

```
4 REM ****************************
5 REM * PROGRAM TO DRAW A BOX *
6 REM ****************************
8 REM
9 REM --SET UP FOUR-COLOR GRAPHICS--
10 GRAPHICS 7
20 COLOR 1
30 REM --GET VALUES FROM KEYBOARD--
40 PRINT "LEFT EDGE";:INPUT XLEFT
50 PRINT "RIGHT EDGE";:INPUT XRIGHT
60 PRINT "TOP";:INPUT YTOP
70 PRINT "BOTTOM";:INPUT YBOTTOM
100 REM
101 REM --MOVE TO UPPER-LEFT CORNER--
110 PLOT XLEFT,YTOP
120 REM
121 REM --DRAW FOUR SIDES OF BOX--
130 DRAWTO XRIGHT,YTOP
140 DRAWTO XRIGHT,YBOTTOM
150 DRAWTO XLEFT,YBOTTOM
160 DRAWTO XLEFT,YTOP

READY
```

Figure 6.7: *The box-drawing program, using INPUT from the keyboard.*

course, you can run the program over again. (If you need to stop the program before you run it over again, press the BREAK key.) Note also that if you type anything other than a number, the computer will object:

```
ERROR-- 8 AT LINE 40
```

When this happens, you will have to RUN the program over from the beginning.

When you finally give your fourth response, the computer will go on to draw the box. If you give the answers shown in Figure 6.8, you will get the same old box as in Figure 6.2. By naming other values in response to your program's questions, you can have the computer draw boxes of any shape.

You have accomplished two important things with this INPUT version of the program. First, you have developed a program which asks you questions as it works. It waits for your responses, and then acts according to your wishes.

Figure 6.8: *At each INPUT statement, the computer asks you what number to use.*

More important, though, you now have a program which you can RUN again and again. Each time you RUN the program it performs the same general task, but the results vary depending on the numbers you supply. This is an important step because your computer is now using its program as a general problem-solver, rather than just as a set of fixed instructions.

DOING CALCULATIONS

You have now seen three different ways you can store numbers in variables. If you just need to assign a value to a single variable, you can use a simple equals sign. If you have several values that you want to store at one time, you might prefer to use the READ and DATA statements. Finally, if you want to supply the value at the time you RUN the program, you can use an INPUT statement.

Up to this point, however, you have been very limited in what you could do with the numbers once you stored them. You could PRINT them, or use them as coordinates in a PLOT or DRAWTO command, but that was about it.

Your computer also allows you to perform calculations on the numbers you have stored. It can add, subtract, multiply, and divide, and can handle more complex mathematical functions as well. All of this is built into the machine: you only need to tell it which formulas to use.

Your computer lets you write your formulas in a way very similar to regular arithmetic. For the standard operations, you use the following symbols:

+ Addition
− Subtraction
* Multiplication
/ Division
^ Exponent ("Power")

The asterisk (*) was chosen for multiplication, since an × might be confusing to the computer. For division the slash (/) is used, because it resembles a fraction bar, which is a form of division. All five of these symbols are located on or near the arrow keys at the right side of the keyboard.

You can write a formula just as you do in arithmetic. You might try typing

```
ANSWER=2+2
```

Your computer will take this very literally, as a command. It takes ANSWER as a variable and looks at the right side of the equals sign for the value it should assign. In this case, it sees 2 + 2, so it calculates the value: 4. Then, it stores this number in the variable to the left of the equal sign: the variable ANSWER. To see that it has indeed been stored, you can type the command

```
PRINT ANSWER
```

Your formulas can be as complicated as you wish, and can contain variable names as well as numbers. You could type any of the following lines:

```
X=15+17
PAY=WAGE*HOURS
AREA=LENGTH*HEIGHT/2
```

In the last of these examples, the formula contains more than two numbers. As in arithmetic, the computer generally calculates formulas from left to right, except that it gives priority to multiplication and division operations. To see how this works, ask the computer to calculate

```
NUMBER=3*4+6/2
```

The computer will calculate the multiplication (3*4) and division (6/2) problems first. Then, it will add the answers together (12 plus 3) and store the result (15).

If you want to override this sequence, or if you simply find this confusing, you can group operations together with parentheses. You could, for instance, write the previous command as follows:

```
NUMBER=(3*4)+(6/2)
```

You will get the same answer. Note that you would get a different answer if you grouped the operations differently:

```
NUMBER=((3*4)+6)/2
```

In this case, the computer will first calculate the multiplication (3*4) in the innermost set of parentheses, then add the answer (12) to the number 6, to solve the outer set of parentheses. Only then will it divide this result by 2 to get the final answer (9). Note that you can put parentheses within a set of parentheses.

If you find these concepts difficult, don't worry. I will stick to very simple equations in this book, so that you won't get lost. If you are comfortable with mathematics, you can certainly learn to write more complicated formulas on your own.

You can use a formula anywhere you would use a number or a variable. You could, for instance, type

```
PRINT 3*5
```

When you press RETURN, the computer will respond with the answer, 15. As you recall, this is very different from

```
PRINT "3*5"
```

Within quotation marks, the computer treats 3*5 as a message to be printed as written, not as a formula to be calculated.

As an example, let's write a program that draws a blue triangle on the screen. (You're getting tired of boxes, aren't you?) As always, press RESET and type NEW before you start. Then type the following program:

```
10  GRAPHICS 7
20  COLOR 2:REM GREEN PAINTBRUSH
30  PRINT "STARTING X";:INPUT X
40  PRINT "STARTING Y";:INPUT Y
50  PLOT X,Y
60  REM MOVE 40 UNITS TO RIGHT
70  DRAWTO X+40,Y
80  REM MOVE DOWN AND TO LEFT
90  DRAWTO X+20,Y+30
100  REM MOVE BACK TO START
110  DRAWTO X,Y
```

When you RUN this program, the computer will ask you for starting X and Y coordinates. The numbers you give will define the point in the upper-left corner of the triangle. Line 50 PLOTs this point, then the rest of the program draws lines to the two other corners, and back to the starting point. The result is a triangle, as shown in Figure 6.9.

RUN the program again, and give different values for the coordinates. In this program, you can use any X up to 119, and any Y up to 49. As you try different combinations, you will find that the triangle always remains the same size and shape, but is moved to different positions on the graphics screen. This happens because all of the coordinates were given relative to the point in the upper-left corner of the triangle. When you change that point, the others will change with it.

STRINGS: STORING LETTERS

As a final topic in this chapter, I will describe a way to store letters in your computer. This is a complex subject, which could easily take up a chapter of its own. I cannot give it that much attention, but I can cover it briefly so that you will understand this concept when you come across it in other books.

You can store words and letters in the computer's memory, just as you can store numbers. To do this, you need a special kind of variable, called a *string variable.* To set up a string variable, you must put a dollar sign ($) at the end of the name. All of these are string variables:

```
A$
NAME$
```

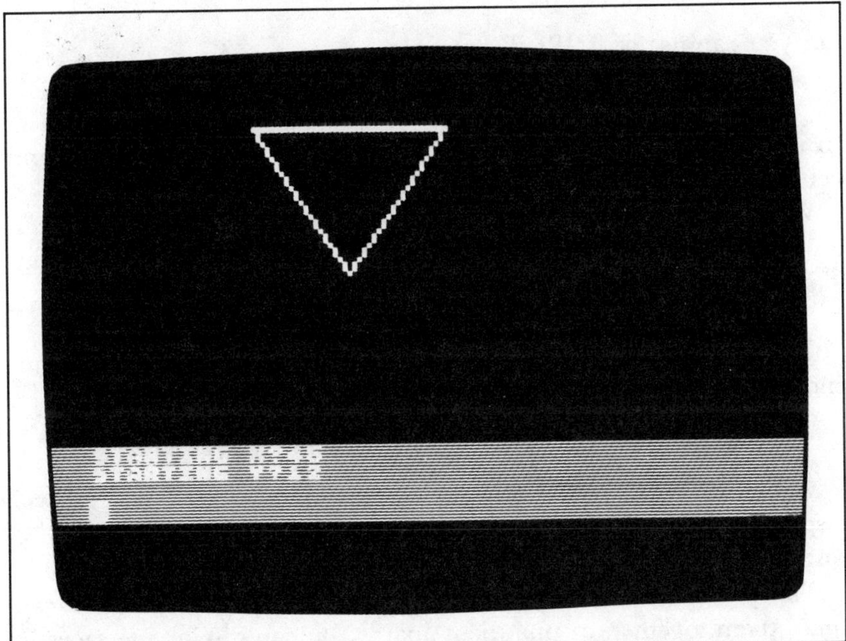

Figure 6.9: *The results of the triangle program.*

```
ADDRESS$
MESSAGE$
```

Before you can use a string variable, you must tell the computer how long the message will be that it is about to store. The computer must know this, so that it can set aside space in its memory for each character in the string. Choose a length longer than you're going to need, then type a statement such as this:

```
10 DIM NAME$(20)
```

DIM stands for "dimension," and this statement tells the computer to set aside space for 20 characters in the string NAME$.

You can now store words or letters in the string variable, just as you stored numbers in normal variables. You can use a standard assignment statement, by enclosing the message in quotes:

```
20 NAME$ = "ARTHUR"
```

You can use a READ and DATA statement:

```
20 READ NAME$
30 DATA ARTHUR
```

Or, you can use an INPUT statement:

```
20 PRINT "WHICH NAME";:INPUT NAME$
```

In the last case, the computer will ask you WHICH NAME?, and you can type ARTHUR from the keyboard.

When you have stored the message in the string variable, you can use it in several ways. You can PRINT it:

```
40 PRINT NAME$
```

You can even use just part of the message by naming the starting and ending letters of the section that you want to use:

```
60 PRINT NAME$(2,4)
```

If you RUN a program with this last statement, the computer will display only the second, third, and fourth letters of the name, in this case RTH.

There are many other things you can do with strings. You can splice them together, or pull them apart. You can display messages in special ways on the screen, or store messages for future use. The applications of this concept are many and varied, but they are a subject for a more advanced book.

OPTIONAL EXERCISES

1. In the version of the box-drawing program shown in Figure 6.7, add an INPUT statement before line 20, so that you can choose a color other than orange. You will need to define a new variable, and will need to modify statement 20.
2. Add statements to the end of the triangle program (Figure 6.9) so that the computer will draw a Star of David. You will need to add PLOT and DRAWTO statements to draw a second triangle on top of the first, with the point facing upward.
3. Store the number 10 in the variable J. Then type the following command:

   ```
   J=J+1
   ```

   What value will J now have? Check your guess by asking the computer to PRINT J.

SUMMARY

In this chapter, you have learned how to use variables, so that you can store a number and reuse it later. Variables let you simplify programs, and make them perform more general operations.

The simplest way to store a number is to set the variable name equal to it. The number will remain stored in that variable until you replace it or turn the computer off.

If you have many numbers to store, or constantly need to change the values you are using, you can READ the values from a DATA statement. Each variable in the READ statement is assigned the corresponding value in the DATA statement. To change the values, you need only change the DATA statement.

The most flexible way to store values is with an INPUT statement. This tells the computer to stop each time it runs the program in order to ask you to type the value at the keyboard. You type the number and press RETURN. The computer then stores the value and continues with the program.

By writing formulas, you can have your computer do calculations for you. The formulas can be as simple or as complex as you wish, and you can easily PRINT the results.

You can store more than just numbers. With string variables, you can store verbal messages as well, and PRINT them out in various ways.

In the chapters ahead, you will learn to use variables and other features to make your computer programs even more flexible and useful.

CHAPTER SEVEN

Controlling Your Program

In the last two chapters, you have learned how to write programs. You can now type commands into the computer and store them as an organized program in its memory. With variables, you can make your programs more flexible, so that they will perform a general task using the values you supply.

Until now, however, you have been locked into the start-to-finish flow of the program. The computer began to RUN the program with the first statement, then went through each of the others in order. When it reached the end of the program, the computer stopped and said READY. It saw each statement only once.

In this chapter, you will learn ways to alter the flow of the program. You can ask the computer to jump from one part of the program to another, or to return to statements it has already used. You can also have the computer do a repetitive task many times, or make decisions based on information you supply. Finally, you will learn how to break your program up into smaller *subprograms,* which you can use as building blocks.

GOTO: *JUMPING TO ANOTHER STATEMENT*

The simplest form of program control is the GOTO statement. This simply tells the computer to jump to another statement in the program and continue from that point. You might, for example, want to jump straight from statement number 20 to 50, skipping any statements in between. You could merely make line 20 a GOTO statement:

```
20  GOTO 50
```

When the computer sees this line, it will immediately skip to line 50 and go on from there. Any lines that fall between 20 and 50 will never be used, unless another GOTO statement sends the computer back to them.

The most common use of GOTO is to send the computer back to the beginning of a group of statements. Try the following program:

```
10  PRINT "HELLO"
20  GOTO 10
```

When you RUN this, your computer will display a vertical column of HELLOs along the left side of the screen.

The computer first encounters line 10, which tells it to display a single word, HELLO. The computer then moves on to line 20. That, however, sends it right back to line 10, so it PRINTs the word again. When it has finished line 10 for the second time, the computer once more proceeds to the next statement. That is line 20 again, which, of course, sends it back to 10. The process goes on and on.

The computer doesn't even stop when it runs out of lines on the screen. If you look carefully at the HELLO on the bottom line, you will see that it is flickering. The computer is still printing the word HELLO repeatedly, and it keeps moving all of the other lines up and off the screen to make room for it.

If you try to type a letter on the keyboard at this point, you will discover that the computer will not accept it. It is still running your program, and all of its attention is directed towards that task. Until the computer finishes a program and says READY, you cannot type any new commands. This is a program, however, which will never end.

This is known as an *infinite loop.* The computer is doing a task over and over again, and will continue until you turn the power off or do something else to stop it. You can stop the program with the RESET key, but that will also erase the screen.

The best way to stop a program is with the BREAK key, located at the upper-right corner of the keyboard on the Atari 600XL and

800XL. When you press this key, the computer will stop in its tracks and say

```
STOPPED AT LINE 10
```

It does not say READY, but the cursor has reappeared to show that you can type letters again.

You will find the BREAK key very useful for stopping programs while they are running. No matter what the computer is doing in your program, the BREAK key will stop it and let you type commands from the keyboard again. This is essential, if you ever get stuck in an infinite loop, or want to cut the program short. If you wish, you can restart the program from the place where you stopped it, by typing the command

```
CONT
```

In most cases, though, you will probably want to use RUN to start over from the beginning.

Infinite loops are not necessarily bad. When you want to do a task over and over, it is often easiest simply to write the program as an infinite loop and stop it manually when you have had enough.

As an example, let's write a program that will double any number that you type in. Try the following program:

```
10 PRINT
20 PRINT "TYPE A NUMBER";:INPUT N
30 PRINT N;" TIMES 2 = ";N*2
40 GOTO 10
```

The program starts by printing a blank line on the screen, to make the display more readable. Line 20 is an INPUT statement that asks you to type a number in from the keyboard. It waits for your response, then puts your number in the variable N. Line 30 then displays first the number N, then the phrase "TIMES 2 = ", and then the answer that it calculates from 2*N. The GOTO statement then sends the computer back to the beginning of the program, to ask you for another number.

The PRINT statement in line 30 may look a little unfamiliar. Up till now, we have only used one variable or one message after the word PRINT. Here we have three: the variable N, the message " TIMES 2 = ", and the answer N*2. The computer understands this perfectly well, and will display the three items one after the other. The semicolons (;) separating the items are important, since they tell the computer to display the three items on the same line with no extra spaces in between.

When you RUN this program, the computer will start by asking you to TYPE A NUMBER. Type 3 and press RETURN. The computer will respond with the answer:

```
3 TIMES 2 = 6
```

It then goes on and asks you to type another number. You can type numbers and have the computer double them as many times as you wish. Figure 7.1 shows how your screen might look after a few more responses. When you're done, press BREAK to regain control of the keyboard.

You can make any program repeat in this way. A good example might be the box-drawing program we developed in Chapter 6.

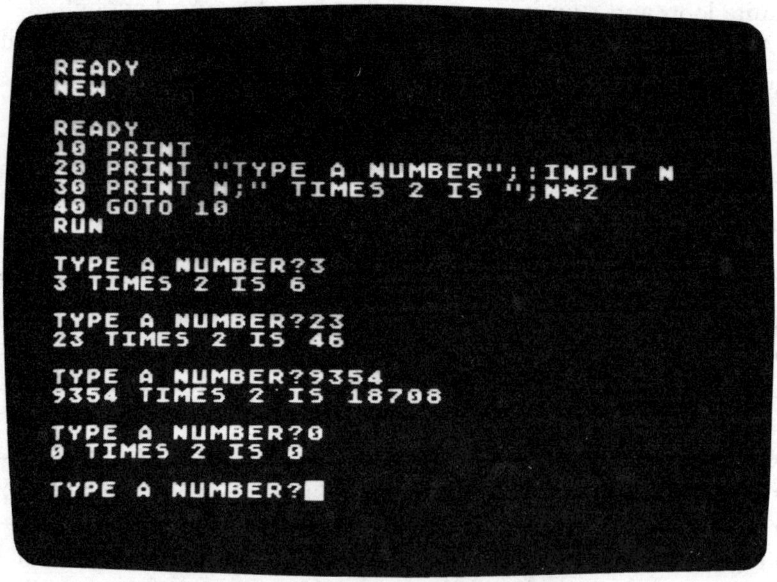

```
READY
NEW

READY
10 PRINT
20 PRINT "TYPE A NUMBER";:INPUT N
30 PRINT N;" TIMES 2 IS ";N*2
40 GOTO 10
RUN

TYPE A NUMBER?3
3 TIMES 2 IS 6

TYPE A NUMBER?23
23 TIMES 2 IS 46

TYPE A NUMBER?9354
9354 TIMES 2 IS 18708

TYPE A NUMBER?0
0 TIMES 2 IS 0

TYPE A NUMBER?█
```

Figure 7.1: *With a GOTO statement, you can have the computer do a task many times.*

Think about what would happen if you added the following line to the program in Figure 6.7:

```
170  GOTO 30
```

The program would RUN as usual, asking you to INPUT the coordinates for the corners of the box. Once you'd typed in four numbers, the computer would immediately draw a yellow box.

Unlike the program in Figure 6.7, however, the computer wouldn't stop when it had finished. Instead, it would go back and ask you for a new set of four numbers. If you typed four more coordinates for the corners, the computer would draw a second box without erasing the first. You could draw as many boxes as you like. Figure 7.2 shows what your screen might look like after four times around the loop.

If you look carefully at the program listing in Figure 6.7, you will notice that this GOTO statement does not send the computer all the way back to the beginning of the program. This is because it is not necessary to repeat the GRAPHICS and COLOR statements in lines

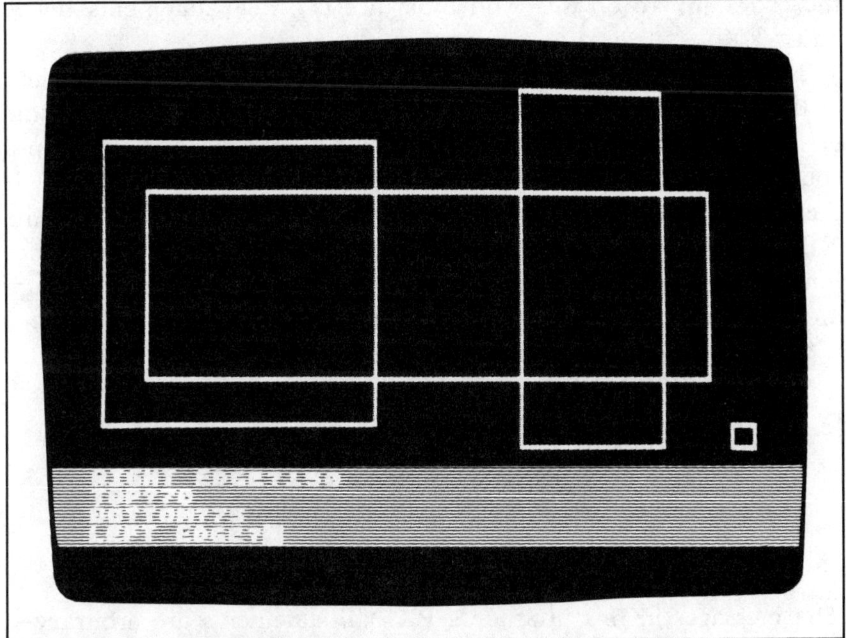

Figure 7.2: *You can modify the box-drawing program so that you can draw more than one box on the screen.*

10 and 20. In fact, the GRAPHICS statement would have cleared the screen each time around and erased the picture we were in the process of building. By using GOTO 30, we repeated only those lines that were necessary.

The GOTO statement is so convenient that many people overuse it. Programs that jump back and forth too much can be very difficult to follow, so you should use this statement only when there is a clear need. People normally expect to read a program from top to bottom, and too many departures from that order can be confusing.

FOR/NEXT *LOOPS*

With the GOTO statement, you have learned how to make the computer repeat a part of your program. The problem is that all of your loops have been infinite: the computer simply repeated the program until you pressed the BREAK key to make it stop.

Often, however, you want to have the computer repeat a group of statements a fixed number of times, then go on to another part of the program. To do this, you must use two new statements: FOR and NEXT.

They work like this. You put the FOR statement at the beginning of the lines you want to repeat, then type a NEXT statement at the end. When the computer comes to the FOR statement, it starts up a counter to keep track of the number of repetitions it has performed. It then keeps repeating all of the statements between the FOR and the NEXT until it reaches the limit you have set. After that it does not jump back when it reaches the NEXT statement, but passes through and continues with the rest of the program.

To see this in action, try the following program:

```
10 PRINT "THE LOOP IS BEGINNING."
20 FOR CNTR=1 TO 10
30 PRINT "REPETITION NO. "; CNTR
40 NEXT CNTR
50 PRINT "THE LOOP IS FINISHED."
```

The messages in this program's PRINT statements are arbitrary—chosen for the purposes of explanation. CNTR is the name chosen for the counter variable, with which the computer keeps track of the repetitions. When you run the program, your results should look like Figure 7.3.

The FOR statement in line 20 tells the computer to repeat the loop a number of times, keeping track with the counter variable named CNTR. The '1 TO 10' in the FOR statement sets the starting and ending values of the counter, and therefore also the number of times to repeat the loop. As you can see from the results of your program, the counter variable starts at 1 on the first pass through the loop, and increases by one each time through. When it reaches the upper limit (10), the counter tells the computer that the loop is done, and the computer proceeds to the statement following the NEXT.

Line 30 shows a useful feature of FOR/NEXT loops:

```
30 PRINT "REPETITION NO.";CNTR
```

Within the loop, you can use the counter as a normal variable. Each time through, CNTR will contain a different value, depending on the number of times the computer has repeated the loop. With careful planning, you can often use this to your advantage.

```
10 PRINT "THE LOOP IS BEGINNING."
20 FOR COUNTER=1 TO 10
30 PRINT "REPETITION NO.";COUNTER
40 NEXT COUNTER
50 PRINT "THE LOOP IS FINISHED."

READY
RUN
THE LOOP IS BEGINNING.
REPETITION NO.1
REPETITION NO.2
REPETITION NO.3
REPETITION NO.4
REPETITION NO.5
REPETITION NO.6
REPETITION NO.7
REPETITION NO.8
REPETITION NO.9
REPETITION NO.10
THE LOOP IS FINISHED.

READY
```

Figure 7.3: *An example of how a FOR/NEXT loop can be used to repeat a PRINT statement.*

The counter variable does not need to start from 1. You can choose any numbers you want for the starting and ending values—even negative numbers. Try some other values in line 20 of this program, such as the following:

```
20 FOR CNTR=7 TO 14

20 FOR CNTR=329 TO 364

20 FOR CNTR= -3 TO 6

20 FOR CNTR=8 TO 5
```

Note that in the last of these examples, the upper limit on the counter was below the starting value. When this happens, the computer goes through the loop only once, then continues past the NEXT statement.

You can also ask the computer to increase the counter each time by some number other than 1. You do this by adding another number to the end of the FOR statement, like this:

```
20 FOR CNTR=1 TO 10 STEP 2
```

If you RUN the program with this statement, you will find that the counter skips by twos: 1, 3, 5, 7, 9. Note that the counter never reaches exactly 10 in this case, but stops the loop at 9, just before it goes over the limit.

You can also use the STEP to make the loop counter go down instead of up. To do this, give the STEP a negative value:

```
20 FOR CNTR=10 TO 1 STEP -1
```

If you run the program in this way, the counter will start with the value 10. When it reaches the end of the loop, it will add −1 to the counter, effectively subtracting one from it. The loop will then repeat with the values 9, 8, and so forth. When it reaches 1, the loop will end and the program will continue.

You can give the counter variable any name you want. You must make sure, however, that you make the name in the FOR statement exactly match the name you use in the NEXT statement to end the loop. If you don't, you get an ERROR. Many people choose to give simple names to their FOR/NEXT counters—especially one-letter names such as I, J, and K.

You can have any group of statements within your loop—even another loop. Try out the following program:

```
10  PRINT "THE LOOPS ARE BEGINNING"
20  FOR I=1 TO 3
30  PRINT "OUTER LOOP --" ;I
40  FOR J=1 TO 4
50  PRINT "INNER LOOP --" ;J
60  NEXT J
70  PRINT "INNER LOOP IS FINISHED"
80  NEXT I
90  PRINT "BOTH LOOPS ARE FINISHED"
```

The results of this program are shown in Figure 7.4. As you can see, the outer loop is repeated three times in the course of the program, each time printing the value of its counter variable, I. Each time through this outer loop, however, the computer encounters the inner loop, with a different counter variable, J. This tells it to repeat the PRINT statement in line 50 four times on each of its three passes through the outer loop.

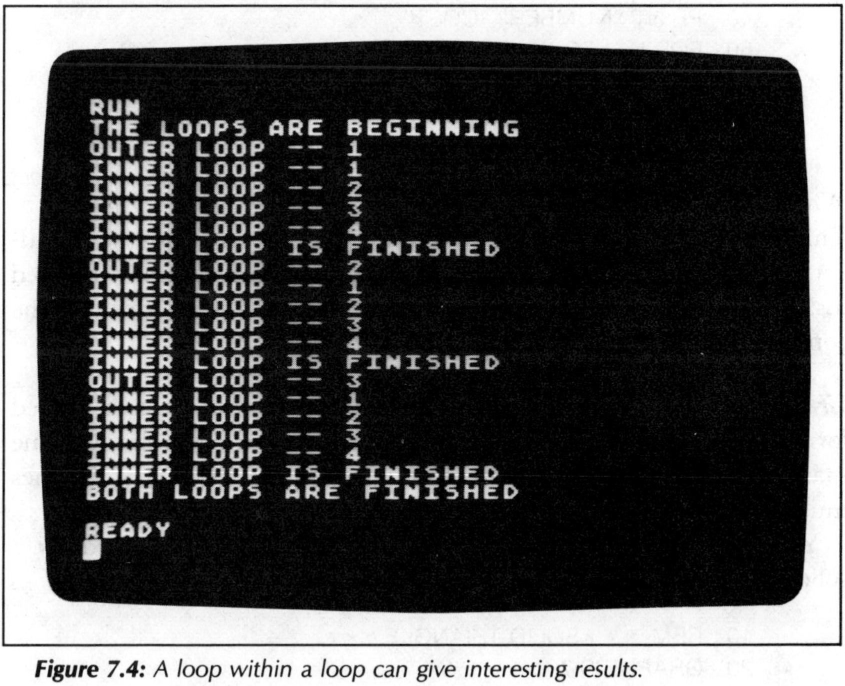

```
RUN
THE LOOPS ARE BEGINNING
OUTER LOOP -- 1
INNER LOOP -- 1
INNER LOOP -- 2
INNER LOOP -- 3
INNER LOOP -- 4
INNER LOOP IS FINISHED
OUTER LOOP -- 2
INNER LOOP -- 1
INNER LOOP -- 2
INNER LOOP -- 3
INNER LOOP -- 4
INNER LOOP IS FINISHED
OUTER LOOP -- 3
INNER LOOP -- 1
INNER LOOP -- 2
INNER LOOP -- 3
INNER LOOP -- 4
INNER LOOP IS FINISHED
BOTH LOOPS ARE FINISHED

READY
```

Figure 7.4: *A loop within a loop can give interesting results.*

There is only one restriction on this useful idea of a loop within a loop: the inner loop must be entirely contained within the outer, like the pieces of a Russian doll. You must make very sure that the NEXT of the inner loop comes before the NEXT of the outer loop, as in the above program. Otherwise you will get an ERROR.

FOR/NEXT loops are useful for almost every type of program. Most programs need to repeat statements in some way, and for many tasks it is essential. Here are some examples of ways you can use FOR/NEXT loops:

Calculations Many computations have to be done over and over again. Often, you need to have a whole list of answers to the same simple problem, and you'd rather not have to calculate it each time.

Suppose, for instance, that you wanted to buy a number of gadgets at $11.39 apiece. You'd like to buy several, but the number you buy will depend on the cost. So, you write a program to make up a table:

```
10 REM ***TABLE OF GADGET COSTS***
20 PRICE=11.39
30 REM PRINT HEADINGS
40 PRINT "NUMBER","COST"
50 FOR I=1 TO 20
60 COST=I*PRICE
70 PRINT I,COST
80 NEXT I
```

When you RUN this program, you will get a table, as in Figure 7.5. This shows how much you would have to pay for any number of gadgets from 1 to 20. Notice that in lines 40 and 70 a comma was used instead of a semicolon. A comma between PRINT messages tells the computer to arrange numbers neatly in columns.

Graphics For many types of pictures, you must use some controlled form of repetition, so that you don't have to plot every point and line manually. Any figure that cannot be made up of a few straight lines must be drawn using a FOR/NEXT loop.

You will need to use a FOR/NEXT loop if you want to draw a solid figure. To see how this works, try the following program:

```
10 REM ***SOLID TRIANGLE***
20 GRAPHICS 7
```

```
30  COLOR 1
40  FOR Y=0 TO 79
50  PLOT 0,Y
60  DRAWTO Y,Y
70  NEXT Y
```

This program steps through every possible value of Y, from 0 at the top of the screen to 79 at the bottom. At each Y, it PLOTs a point at the left edge of the screen (coordinate 0,Y), then draws a horizontal line Y units long. The result is a solid triangular region, as shown in Figure 7.6.

Delays Each time the computer has to repeat a FOR/NEXT loop, it wastes a fraction of a second. In most programs, you will hardly notice this delay. If you ask for a large number of repetitions, though, the time begins to add up.

You can use this to your advantage when you want to slow down

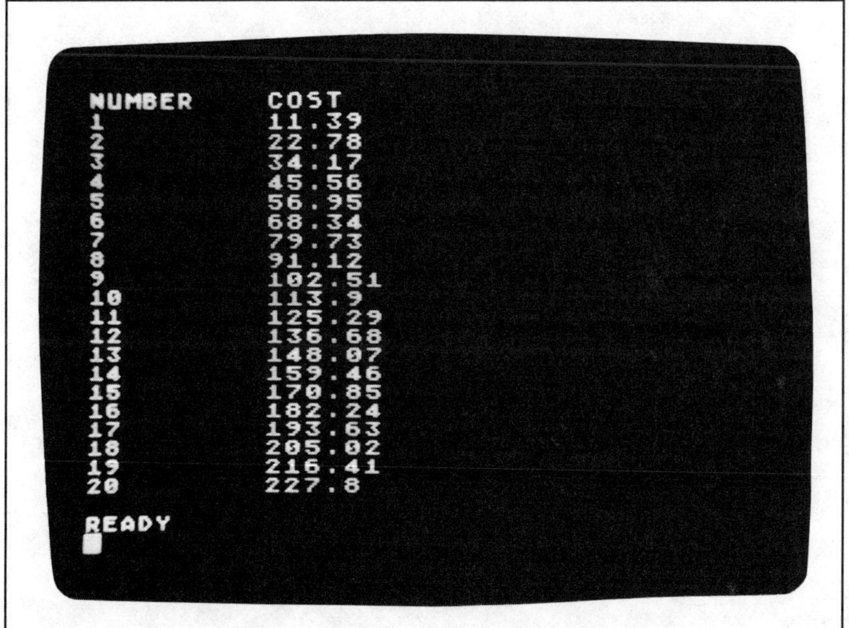

Figure 7.5: *You can create a table with a FOR/NEXT loop.*

the action or have the computer pause. Write a FOR/NEXT loop with many repetitions at the place where you want the pause:

```
20 FOR DELAY=1 TO 5000
30 NEXT DELAY
```

This loop does nothing whatsoever as it goes through its 5000 repetitions; however, it wastes about ten seconds in the process. This might be helpful in a program such as this:

```
10 PRINT "PATIENCE TEST"
20 FOR DELAY=1 TO 5000
30 NEXT DELAY
40 PRINT "YOU PASSED!"
```

When you RUN this program, the computer immediately displays the words

```
PATIENCE TEST
```

It then goes into the "do-nothing loop" and waits about 10 seconds before congratulating you.

Figure 7.6: *You can draw solid regions on the screen, using FOR/NEXT loops.*

Delay loops are common in many Atari programs. Since the FOR and NEXT statements here are really a single idea, many people write them on a single line, separated by a colon:

```
20 FOR DELAY=1 TO 5000:NEXT DELAY
```

In these and other uses, FOR/NEXT loops give you a new range of control over your computer. They let you repeat a group of statements any number of times, then go on to the next part of the program. While the computer is repeating the loop, it also keeps track of a counter variable, which you can use in your calculations. You will find more and more uses for these statements as you explore the capabilities of your computer.

IF STATEMENTS: MAKING DECISIONS

You can also control the way the computer runs your program by having it make decisions. With the IF statement, you can have the machine decide whether or not to do something depending on the values of certain variables.

Of course, the computer isn't making an independent decision. You tell it to do one thing if a certain condition is met, and another thing if it isn't. It makes its choice in response to the information you give it. The computer doesn't really think; it just follows the course that fits the conditions.

The IF statement consists of two parts: a condition and a response. The two parts of the statement are signalled by the words IF and THEN. The general form of the statement is

```
10 IF condition THEN response
```

When you actually write this statement, you will replace the words *condition* and *response* with a specific comparison and command.

The condition will usually be a comparison between a variable and some numbers. You could, for example, test to see if the variable NUMBER is equal to 0. You would start by writing

```
10 IF NUMBER=0 THEN . . .
```

The computer would check the value stored in NUMBER. If it is exactly 0, the computer will carry out the response. If it is not, the computer will skip the response and proceed to the next statement in the program.

You can use a variety of arithmetic comparisons in your IF condition. The most important are

=	equal to
>	greater than
>=	greater than or equal to
<	less than
<=	less than or equal to
<>	not equal to

You can also combine two or more conditions with the words AND and OR. If you wanted to see if a number was more than 5 and less than 10, you could use the condition

```
10  IF NUMBER>5 AND NUMBER<10 THEN . . .
```

The computer would carry out the response only if the variable NUMBER had a value between 5 and 10.

The response, which follows the word THEN in the statement, can be any Atari command. If the condition in the IF part is satisfied, the computer will follow the command; if the condition isn't satisfied, it will pass the command by.

Here are some examples of valid IF statements:

```
10  IF I=10 THEN PRINT "NUMBER IS TEN"
20  IF MODE=0 THEN GRAPHICS 0
30  IF SIZE>20 THEN SIZE=20
```

Line 10 will display a message on the screen if at that point the variable I is equal to ten. If I has any other value, no message is displayed. Line 20 uses an IF statement to reset the computer to GRAPHICS mode 0 (standard text), if it discovers the variable MODE has been given the value 0.

Line 30 shows a common use of the IF statement. When it arrives at this statement, the computer checks to see if the variable SIZE has exceeded 20. If it has, the computer resets it to 20. After this statement, you can be certain that SIZE will not be greater than this maximum value.

To see the IF statement in action, let's try a simple program that lets you guess at a number from 1 to 100. Type in this program:

```
10  ANSWER=57
20  PRINT
30  REM BLANK LINE
40  PRINT "TYPE A NUMBER FROM 1 TO 100"
50  INPUT N
60  IF N<ANSWER THEN PRINT "TOO SMALL"
70  IF N>ANSWER THEN PRINT "TOO BIG"
80  IF N=ANSWER THEN PRINT "CORRECT!"
90  GOTO 20
```

Line 10 of this program gives the correct answer to the computer. The rest of the program is an infinite loop that asks you to type a number, then compares it to the correct answer.

When you RUN this program, the computer will start by asking you to

```
TYPE A NUMBER FROM 1 TO 100
```

You know the answer (57), but try some other numbers too. Give your response and press RETURN. The computer will say either TOO SMALL, TOO LARGE, or CORRECT, depending on the number that you type. The computer makes its choice according to the IF statements in lines 60 through 80, then PRINTs the appropriate response. Line 90 sends the computer back to the beginning of the loop, to ask for another number. Figure 7.7 shows the results of several guesses. When you have finished, press BREAK to stop the program.

You can make the computer expect a different answer, merely by changing line 10. You might even enjoy playing this as a game. Store a number in the computer by typing it into line 10, then clear the screen and RUN the program. You can then have a friend try to guess the number that you typed in.

IF statements are often used to ask the computer to GOTO another part of the program only under a certain condition. You could, for example, have the number-guessing program go back to line 20 only if the answer was wrong. Replace the simple GOTO statement in line 90 with the following IF statement:

```
90  IF N<>ANSWER THEN GOTO 20
```

The <> is a "not equals" condition, and will send the computer on two different paths through the program, depending on whether the values of the variables N and ANSWER are equal or not. If they are not equal, the computer will jump directly back to line 20 and continue from there. If the numbers are equal, however, the condition will be false, and the computer will skip the GOTO command. Normally, it would then continue with the next statement, but since this is the last line, the program simply ends.

IF statements with a GOTO response allow you to split your program into two parts, then let the computer choose which path to take, depending on the circumstances. You might, for example, write a program such as this:

```
10  PRINT "TYPE A NUMBER";:INPUT N
20  IF N=0 THEN GOTO 50
30  PRINT "STATEMENT 30 IS USED"
40  GOTO 10
50  PRINT "STATEMENT 50 IS USED"
60  GOTO 10
```

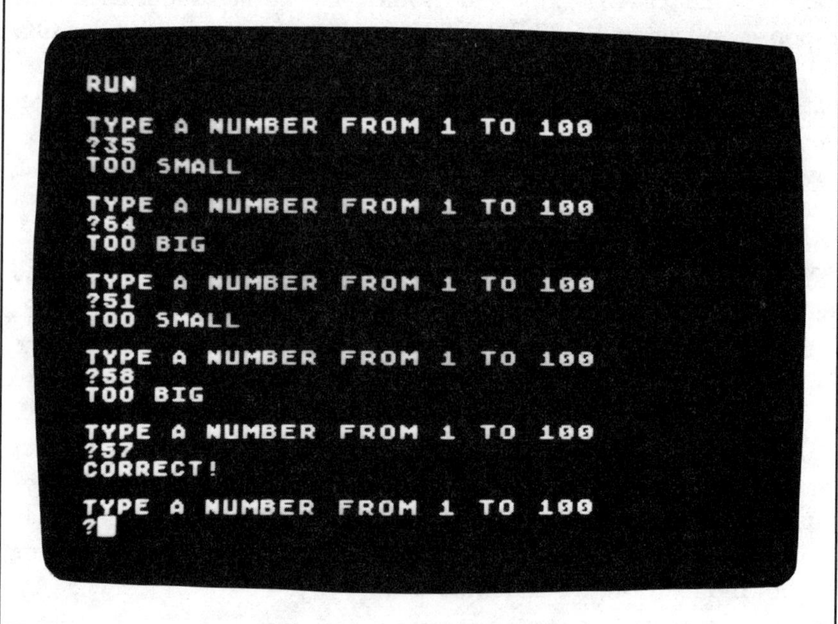

Figure 7.7: *Results of the number-guessing program.*

This program asks for a number, then tests to see if it is zero. If it is, the computer jumps to statement 50 and prints a message. If the number is not zero, the computer bypasses the response and continues with the next statement, number 30. In either case, the computer returns to line 10 after it PRINTs the message.

The IF statement lets you use a technique called *data checking*. Often when you write a program that asks for input from the keyboard, you are expecting a response of a certain kind. You might, for instance, expect a number from 1 to 12, to represent a month of the year. You can guard against meaningless responses by making a simple check:

```
10  PRINT "WHICH MONTH";:INPUT MONTH
20  IF MONTH<1 OR MONTH>12 THEN GOTO 10
30  PRINT "OK"
```

When you RUN this program, the computer will ask you to type a number to represent a month. If the value is meaningless, however, the IF statement will send the computer back to line 10 to ask for another value. It will keep doing this until you type a number between 1 and 12. In any statements you might add after line 30, you can be sure that the variable has a value that represents an actual month.

IF statements clearly have many other uses. Whenever you want your computer to do more than a simple task, you will need to have it make decisions along the way. With the IF statement, you can easily control the way it makes these choices.

GOSUB: *SUBPROGRAMS*

There is another important way you can change the start-to-finish flow of your program. This is with *subprograms*, a series of statements which you can set off from the rest of your program and use as a unit whenever you want.

To use a subprogram, you must *call* it with a GOSUB statement, such as this:

```
40  GOSUB 1000
```

This acts just like a GOTO statement, sending the computer to line number 1000 to continue its work. With GOSUB, however, you tell the computer that you want it to come back after it has finished using the subprogram.

The subprogram itself is like any other group of statements, except that it ends with the command RETURN. When the computer gets to this final command, it sees that the subprogram is done, and goes back to the statement following the original GOSUB. In this way, you can tell the computer to go off and follow a group of instructions, then come back to the point where it left off.

To see how this works, let's try a sample program:

```
10  PRINT "MAIN PROGRAM BEGINS"
20  GOSUB 1000
30  PRINT "MAIN PROGRAM CONTINUES"
40  END
1000  REM SAMPLE SUBPROGRAM
1010  PRINT "NOW RUNNING SUBPROGRAM"
1020  RETURN
```

When you RUN this program, the computer will respond like this:

```
MAIN PROGRAM BEGINS
NOW RUNNING SUBPROGRAM
MAIN PROGRAM CONTINUES
```

From this you can trace the flow of the program. The computer began with line 10, the beginning of the main program. At line 20, it jumped to the subprogram and printed the second message. At the RETURN statement, however, the computer finished the subprogram and went back to the main program, continuing with line 30, which immediately follows the GOSUB statement that called the subprogram.

The END command in line 40 is quite important. It signals the end of the main program and tells the computer to stop. If this statement were not there, the computer would continue running the program, going on to line 1000 of the subprogram, which would be the next line. This would not be what you wanted, unless you did in fact want it to rerun the subprogram at the end of the main one.

You can have many different subprograms, as long as each has different statement numbers and ends with a RETURN. While you are free to choose any statement numbers for your subprograms, you will find it best to use rather high numbers, such as the 1000 chosen here. In that way you leave space in case you later decide to expand your main program. Also, it is generally best to start each subprogram with a remark (REM statement), that describes what the subprogram does.

You can put any kind of statement in a subprogram. You can even use another GOSUB statement to call a second subprogram. If you do this, the RETURN statement from the second subprogram will send the computer back to the GOSUB statement in the first. The computer will go on from there to complete the first subprogram, then return to finish up the main program.

You may be tempted to use a GOTO rather than a RETURN to get back to the main program. Don't. There is a way you can do this, but you will usually end up confusing both yourself and your computer. Make your subprograms self-contained, and be careful to have them RETURN when they are done.

Why use subprograms? There are a variety of reasons why you might want to break up your program into smaller parts. Here are a few:

- *To use a group of statements more than once.* In large programs, you often have certain tasks which you need to do over and over. If you just want to repeat the group a number of times in one place, you might be able to use a FOR/NEXT loop. If, however, you need to reuse the group at another part of your program, you would need to type the FOR/NEXT loop over again at each point where you want to use it. Instead of doing this, you can group the statements together in a subprogram. Then, each time you need to do the task, you can call it with a simple GOSUB statement.
- *To make a program modular.* Very long programs can seem terribly daunting if you try to view them all at once. By breaking the program down into more manageable units, you can make it much easier to understand. Some people write their main programs as a series of GOSUB statements, which direct the computer to each of the modules in turn.
- *To develop a subprogram library.* At some point, you might want to put together a collection of subprograms that you often use as building blocks for different kinds of programs.

If you store all of these routines on a cassette or diskette, you can load any one of them back into the computer whenever you want to use it in a program.

With subprograms, we have reached the end of our exploration of the statements that control the flow of your program. With the statements you have learned in this chapter, you are well on your way toward programming your computer effectively.

OPTIONAL EXERCISES

1. Write a program that will ask for a number, then say whether it was positive, negative, or zero. You will need an INPUT and an IF statement. Remember that you use a minus sign to type a negative number.
2. Write a subprogram that clears the screen by PRINTing ESC and CONTROL/CLEAR. Then tack it on to one of your other programs to improve the appearance of the screen display.
3. Write a FOR/NEXT loop to calculate the sum of the numbers from 1 to 100. Hint: set up a variable SUM and add the counter variable to it each time through the loop.

SUMMARY

In this chapter, you have learned many new ways to control your computer. You are no longer locked into a simple top-to-bottom march through your program; you can jump around, turn loops, make decisions, and run subprograms.

The GOTO statement tells the computer to jump to another statement. You can jump forward or backward within your program, and create infinite loops if you wish. This is often a simple way to do repetitive tasks.

With FOR and NEXT statements, you can make your computer repeat a group of statements a certain number of times, then go on to the rest of the program.

IF statements let your computer make decisions in the course of your program. At any point, you can tell the computer to test a condition. If the condition is true, your IF statement will have the computer take some action. It can print a message, change a value, or go to another part of the program—anything you choose.

The GOSUB statement gives you yet another way to determine the flow of your program. You can break a large program up into smaller blocks, then use the blocks whenever you need them. This lets you write simpler programs, which you can work with one piece at a time.

With this chapter, you have come to the end of the standard programming techniques covered in this book. Chapter 8 is a whirlwind tour of the advanced graphics features of your Atari computer, which will show you some more of its potential.

CHAPTER EIGHT

Advanced Graphics

In Chapter 4, you learned a little about the Atari graphics system. You learned how to use the POSITION statement to place text messages anywhere on the screen. You found out how to plot points and draw lines in the four-color graphics mode, creating pictures with your computer.

In this chapter, you will learn more about the Atari graphics system. You will learn how to control the colors of the screen background and the graphics paintbrushes. You will find out how to eliminate the text window at the bottom of the screen, so you can draw larger pictures. Finally, in a tour of the other graphics modes, you will discover other ways to control the screen display.

In these few pages, I cannot describe the entire Atari graphics system. Instead, I have made this a whirlwind tour to give at least a taste of some of the wonderful things you can do with your Atari graphics. If you would like a more complete description, consult one of the more technical books devoted to the Atari.

This chapter deals with difficult subjects. The deeper points of the Atari graphics system are very interesting, but they can be confusing at first. Don't worry if you get hung up from time to time. Just go on to the rest of the book, and come back when you feel you understand better.

CHANGING COLORS WITH **SETCOLOR**

So far, you have used only a few colors: the white and blue letters and background, and the four graphics paintbrushes (orange, green, blue, and black). Your computer has a range of 16 colors to choose from. Within each of the 16 colors, you can select 16 *luminances,* or shades. So in effect, you have 256 colors at your disposal. Even if you are using a black-and-white television, you will be able to control the brightness of the gray tones.

You have been using the COLOR command to choose among the four graphics paintbrushes, but you have not been able to change the preset color that was assigned to each one (orange, green, blue, and black). You could choose your colors to some extent by switching paintbrushes, but you did not have full control.

The COLOR command has a companion called SETCOLOR, which assigns any colors you choose to the four paintbrushes. You could, for example, make the first paintbrush white instead of orange. While you cannot use more than four colors at one time, you can choose those four from any of the 256 possibilities available.

Don't confuse COLOR with SETCOLOR. COLOR chooses which of the four paintbrushes you will be using. So when you ask for COLOR 2, you are really asking for paintbrush 2. You can think of it as saying, "Pick up this paintbrush and keep using it until I tell you otherwise." SETCOLOR, on the other hand, sets the color of paint that will be found on each paintbrush. It says, in effect, "Wash out this paintbrush and dip it in a new color." Unlike an ordinary paintbrush, however, SETCOLOR also goes back and changes the color of all the points that brush has already painted on the screen.

The SETCOLOR command always contains three numbers, in a form such as this:

```
SETCOLOR 2,9,4
```

Each of the three numbers that follows the word SETCOLOR has a special meaning. Figure 8.1 gives a quick-reference chart for using the three numbers in the four-color graphics mode.

The first number (A) names the *color register* you want to change. A color register is a place where the computer can store a code that controls one of the colors on the screen. Once stored, the new code changes the color of the paintbrush attached to that register, without affecting any of the others.

The Atari computers have five color registers, numbered 0 through 4. Unfortunately, the registers have different meanings, depending on which graphics mode you are using. For instance, Register 2 sets the color of a paintbrush in four-color graphics, but in text mode it merely controls the background. It would be quite difficult to learn the meanings for all of the modes, but you can easily master the most important ones.

The first column of Figure 8.1 shows the meaning of each of the registers in the four-color graphics mode. Note that the registers in the SETCOLOR command are numbered differently from the "paint-brush numbers" you have been using in your COLOR statements. (This may seem confusing, but you can understand it if you remember that the "erasebrush" is always 0 in the COLOR statement, and always the *last* of the four SETCOLOR registers number 4.) Figure 8.2 shows the correspondence of the COLOR and SETCOLOR codes, along with the preset colors of the five registers. Just find the paintbrush you want in the COLOR column, then use the corresponding SETCOLOR register to change it. Register 3 (red) is not used in this mode, but is important for some of the others. The preset colors of the registers are the same in every mode.

The second number in your SETCOLOR command controls the

SETCOLOR A, B, C		
A: COLOR REGISTER	**B:** COLOR (HUE)	**C:** LUMINANCE
0—Paintbrush #1 1—Paintbrush #2 2—Paintbrush #3 3—(unused) 4—Erasebrush (#0) and background	0—Gray 1—Light orange (gold) 2—Orange 3—Red-orange 4—Pink 5—Pink-purple 6—Purple-blue 7—Blue 8—Light blue 9—Blue-green 10—Turquoise 11—Green-blue 12—Green 13—Yellow-green 14—Orange-green 15—Light orange	0—Very dim 2— 4— 6— 8— Medium 10— 12— 14—Very bright

Figure 8.1: *The codes for the three numbers in the SETCOLOR command in the four-color graphics mode.*

color. In this mode you may choose from the sixteen colors shown in column B of Figure 8.1. You will notice that the colors are arranged like an endless rainbow. If you move through the colors from 0 to 15 and back to 0, you will see them go through an almost continuous cycle. This is often useful in programs.

The third number in the SETCOLOR command sets the *luminance,* or brightness of the color. For any of the sixteen colors, you can choose from eight different shades. The lowest, 0, is almost black, while the highest, 14, is very bright. In between, you can adjust the brightness to fit your needs. Note that in this mode your computer accepts only even numbers for the luminance setting. If you use an odd number, it will be rounded down.

To see how all this works in practice, let's change the colors of the paintbrushes. To get some lines painted with the three paintbrushes, type the following program into your computer:

```
10 GRAPHICS 7
20 COLOR 1
30 FOR Y=10 TO 20
40 PLOT 20,Y
50 DRAWTO 140,Y
60 NEXT Y
70 COLOR 2
80 FOR Y=30 TO 40
90 PLOT 20,Y
100 DRAWTO 140,Y
110 NEXT Y
120 COLOR 3
130 FOR Y=50 TO 60
140 PLOT 20,Y
150 DRAWTO 140,Y
160 NEXT Y
```

When you RUN this program, your computer will shift into the four-color graphics mode and draw three wide horizontal bands on the screen. Each band is drawn with a different paintbrush in its preset color: one orange, one green, and one blue. In the text window at the bottom of the screen, the computer says READY to show that it has finished.

Now that you have regions painted with each of the three brushes, you can change their color settings. Let's first change paintbrush 1 from orange to some other color. Type the following command:

```
SETCOLOR 0,5,12
```

When you press RETURN, the orange bar will turn to a bright pink. The first number names the register you are changing: register 0, which controls paintbrush number 1. The other two numbers name the color and the brightness you are changing that register to; color 5 (pink-purple), with a brightness of 12.

Try changing either the color or the brightness of this first bar, using other SETCOLOR 0 commands. Also, change the colors of the other two paintbrushes with SETCOLOR 1 and SETCOLOR 2 commands. Don't be surprised if some of these commands also affect the text window. In changing paintbrushes, you are also changing the text and background colors of the bottom of the screen. There is no way to change one without the other.

You can change the color of the screen background by changing the SETCOLOR 4 register. Try typing this, for example:

```
SETCOLOR 4,5,6
```

The entire background of the screen will change to pink. This changes the color drawn by the erasebrush, paintbrush 0, to pink as well, since erasure is simply painting over with the background color.

If you get tired of your new colors, you can return the machine to its preset colors. Use the values shown in the right column of Figure 8.2:

```
SETCOLOR 0,2,8
SETCOLOR 1,12,10
```

SETCOLOR REGISTER	PAINTBRUSH NUMBER (COLOR)	PRESET COLOR	SETCOLOR CODE
0	COLOR 1	Orange	0,2,8
1	COLOR 2	Green	1,12,10
2	COLOR 3	Blue	2,9,4
3	—	Pink or Red	3,4,6
4	COLOR 0 (erase)	Black	4,0,0

Figure 8.2: *The COLOR and SETCOLOR codes in the four-color graphics mode.*

```
SETCOLOR 2,9,4
SETCOLOR 4,0,0
```

These are called the *default values,* because they are the codes that are stored in the color registers when you turn your machine on. You can get back to these codes by pressing RESET as well, though that will also clear the screen.

You can also use SETCOLOR to change the appearance of the screen in the regular text mode (GRAPHICS 0). The SETCOLOR registers have different meanings in this mode, but they are no more difficult. Instead of controlling paintbrushes, the registers in the text mode control regions of the screen—text, background, and border. Figure 8.3 shows their meanings.

Register 1 controls only the luminance of the letters, not their color. The letters are always the same color as the background: you can set them lighter or darker, but never to a different hue.

To see how this works, press RESET to return the color registers to their original state. The default setting of the background color, shown in Figure 8.3, is color 9 with a brightness of 4—dark blue. The letters of the word READY are set by register 1, which starts out as color 12 and brightness 10, which would normally be light green. The computer, however, ignores the color and uses only the brightness (10), making the letters light blue, rather than green. When the letters have a brightness less than the screen background, they show up dark against a lighter background.

Try changing the colors of the letters, background, and screen border. Here are some interesting combinations:

```
SETCOLOR 2,0,0
SETCOLOR 2,15,14
```

SETCOLOR REGISTER	REGION OF SCREEN	PRESET COLOR	SETCOLOR CODE
0	—	Orange	0,2,8
1	Text Luminance	Green	1,12,10
2	Background	Blue	2,9,4
3	—	Pink or Red	3,4,6
4	Border	Black	4,0,0

Figure 8.3: *The SETCOLOR registers in the text mode.*

```
SETCOLOR 2,9,4
SETCOLOR 1,0,14
SETCOLOR 1,0,0
SETCOLOR 4,5,10
```

You can always press RESET to return to the blue screen.

If, at any point, you change the letters and the screen background so that they have the same brightness value, the letters will seem to disappear. They are still there, but you cannot distinguish them from the screen around them. To get them back, press RESET or blindly type another SETCOLOR command.

ELIMINATING THE TEXT WINDOW

In all of your graphics programs, a blue window has remained for text at the bottom of the screen. This is important, because if the computer used the whole screen for graphics, you would have no place to type your commands.

At times, however, you will want to draw pictures that cover the entire screen. Full-screen pictures are generally more attractive, since they are not disrupted by the blue region. Also, some of the more advanced graphics modes cannot be used with a text window.

You ask the computer to remove the text window simply by adding 16 to the mode number in the GRAPHICS statement:

```
10 GRAPHICS 7+16
```

Since 7 + 16 equals 23, you could also write this:

```
10 GRAPHICS 23
```

It is better to write 7 + 16, though, because this makes it clearer what you are doing.

Since the graphics will now extend below the bottom of the regular graphics screen, you can use some coordinates that are larger than normal. The limits on x are the same as before (0 to 159), but the y-coordinates can now run as high as 95 (rather than the usual 79).

Since these extended graphics screens leave you no space to type commands, you can use them only in programs. You must write commands into your program for everything you want the computer to draw, then type the RUN command. Once the computer switches into this kind of graphics mode, you can no longer give direct commands.

If you let your program end normally, the computer will not leave your picture on the screen, as it usually does. Instead, it will erase the entire picture immediately, to make room for the word READY. To prevent this, send the computer into an infinite loop with the last statement in the program, so that it draws the picture and then gets stuck. You do this with a statement such as this:

```
999 GOTO 999
```

When the computer gets to this final statement, it will simply stop, with your picture frozen on the screen.

The computer still won't respond to what you type on the keyboard: it is busy repeating line 999. When you're ready to give commands again, press the BREAK key to stop the program. This will erase the picture from the screen and let you type commands again.

Try the following program to see how full-screen graphics work:

```
10 GRAPHICS 7+16
20 COLOR 1
30 PLOT 0,0
40 DRAWTO 159,95
50 PLOT 0,95
60 DRAWTO 159,0
999 GOTO 999
```

When you RUN the program, the computer should draw an orange X across the entire screen. Line 999 locks it in an infinite loop, so that the picture will remain on the screen. Press BREAK to regain control.

THE GRAPHICS MODES

So far you have seen only two of your computer's sixteen graphics modes. These are the most important, but the other fourteen are also useful. By using the mode that exactly suits your purposes, you can design your graphic displays just the way you want them.

Figure 8.4 is a comparison chart that shows what each of the modes does. Look carefully at the differences between the modes.

The *resolution* column is very important. This pair of numbers tells how many rows and columns the screen is divided into. The higher the resolution, the finer your points and lines can be. If you want to draw very detailed pictures, then you will want the highest possible resolution. On the other hand, if you want to draw pictures with thick lines, you can use lower resolution modes.

The resolution you choose also affects the amount of memory you use. In high-resolution graphics modes, the computer must use substantial memory space to store the information it needs to paint the picture. This is very important if you have an Atari 600XL without memory expansions, because some of the modes will take up almost the entire available memory. This can cause problems, because in these modes you may not be able to write programs longer than ten or fifteen lines. You can use all of the graphics modes on your machine, but you must be very careful with modes that use more than 8000 bytes of memory (see the right column of Figure 8.4). Memory is not a problem if you have a memory expansion or one of the more expensive Atari computers, such as the 800XL.

If you have any of the new XL series computers, you have all sixteen modes. If you have one of the older Atari 400 or 800 computers, you lack some of the modes between 9 and 15. All of the old computers have modes 0 through 8, and some of the later ones have 9,

MODE NUMBER	TYPE OF MODE	RESOLUTION	NUMBER OF COLORS	MEMORY USED (BYTES)
0	Normal text	40 × 24	1	992
1	Large text	20 × 20	5	674
2	Large text	20 × 10	5	424
3	4-color graphics	40 × 20	4	434
4	2-color graphics	80 × 40	2	694
5	4-color graphics	80 × 40	4	1174
6	2-color graphics	160 × 80	2	2174
7	4-color graphics	160 × 80	4	4190
8	High-res. graphics	320 × 160	1	8112
9	GTIA graphics	80 × 192	1	8138
10	GTIA graphics	80 × 192	9	8138
11	GTIA graphics	80 × 192	16	8138
12	4-color text	40 × 20	5	1154
13	4-color text	40 × 10	5	664
14	2-color graphics	160 × 160	2	4270
15	4-color graphics	160 × 160	4	8112

Figure 8.4: *The 16 graphics modes.*

10, and 11 as well. Don't worry: even if you lack a few specialized modes, you've got all of the essentials. Just skip the descriptions of the modes you don't have.

With this said, we can proceed with our tour of Atari graphics. In these few pages, unfortunately, I can only give a brief overview. If you want to know more, I'd suggest you read Bill Carris's book *Inside ATARI BASIC* (Reston, 1983), or *Atari Sound and Graphics,* by Moore, Lower, and Albrecht (Wiley, 1982). These go into much greater detail than I can in this book.

Four-color Graphics Modes. You have already been using one of these: graphics mode 7. The other three work in exactly the same way, but they offer different degrees of resolution. Modes 3 and 5 have lower resolution, so their rows and columns are larger and their coordinates smaller.

Mode 15 has even finer resolution than mode 7, with boxes only half as high. Unfortunately, it also takes up twice as much memory—almost the entire space available on the Atari 600XL. If you have an Atari 800XL or a memory expansion, you will find mode 15 very useful.

The paintbrushes and the SETCOLOR registers all work in exactly the same way in these four modes. You can change a program from one mode to the other merely by changing your coordinates to reflect the different scale.

Two-color Graphics Modes. Modes 4, 6, and 14 are identical to the four-color modes 5, 7, and 15, except that they lack two of the four paintbrushes. You can still use paintbrush number 1, which starts out orange, and the erasebrush (COLOR 0); however, you cannot use paintbrushes 2 and 3.

What's the point of the two-color modes if they don't do anything different? They use only half as much space in the computer's memory, which can be important if you are writing a long program on an Atari 600XL. If you only want to paint with one color, you can save space by using these modes.

High-resolution Graphics. Your Atari computer also offers you a special high-resolution graphics mode. This is number 8, and it is quite different from the others.

GRAPHICS 8 gives you twice the resolution of even the finest two- and four-color modes—the points it plots are the smallest that can be displayed on a normal television screen. This means that the computer can draw diagonal lines that look almost exactly straight, without the "staircase effect" you often see in other modes. You can use this higher resolution to draw intricate pictures with fine detail.

You pay a price, though. To achieve this high resolution, you have to sacrifice color: you can only draw lines of the same hue as the screen background. In general, this means you will need to restrict yourself to white.

The high-resolution graphics also take up a great deal of space in the computer's memory. To use this mode on the Atari 600XL, you must either write very simple programs or buy a memory expansion.

You do have some control over screen colors in the high-resolution graphics mode, but the system for changing colors is not the same as in the other graphics modes. Instead, it resembles the standard text mode. SETCOLOR 2 chooses the background color, SETCOLOR 1 chooses the brightness of the plotted points and lines, and SETCOLOR 4 controls the border. As in the text mode, you cannot make the points a different color from the background; you can only control their brightness. The SETCOLOR commands affect the text window as well as the graphics screen.

You really have only one graphics paintbrush in the high-resolution mode, but you can turn it on and off with the COLOR command. COLOR 1 sets the paintbrush so that it draws lines, while COLOR 0 makes it erase by drawing with the background color.

If you want to use high-resolution graphics, I'd suggest you start off with the following sequence of commands:

```
GRAPHICS 8
SETCOLOR 2,0,0
COLOR 1
```

This selects the mode and changes the background color to black, to make the graphics display stand out. You can certainly use other screen colors, but this combination of white-on-black generally works best.

Special Graphics Modes (GTIA). The XL series and some of the more recent Atari 400 and 800 models have three other special graphics modes, numbered 9, 10, and 11. These are sometimes called the *GTIA modes,* after the name of the electronic chip that Atari installed to produce them.

These three modes are useful because they offer a wider range of colors. In one of them, 11, you can have sixteen different hues on the screen at once, which allows you to produce rainbow-like displays. In another, mode 9, you can display 16 different shades of brightness all at once.

The GTIA modes plot points that are slightly wider than the normal graphics modes. While this is not a serious restriction on resolution, it makes it difficult to draw thin diagonal lines realistically. These modes are therefore better for pictures that fill whole regions of the screen with color.

The GTIA modes are unfortunately rather hard to use, because they work quite differently from the others. The wider range of color choices makes the SETCOLOR statement more complicated, and gives strange meanings to the paintbrush numbers in the COLOR statement. Also, since these three modes do not preserve a text window at the bottom of the screen, they can be used only in programs.

Mode number 11 is perhaps the most impressive of the three. All of the points you plot must be of the same luminance, but you can use all 16 of the hues at once. You set the luminance of all the points by putting a value into SETCOLOR register 4. You can then choose from 16 different paintbrushes with the COLOR statement. The paintbrushes are numbered 0 through 15, to match the color codes in the middle column of Figure 8.1.

Mode number 9 is a one-color version of the same idea. In this mode, all of your points will be the same color, but you can use all 16 luminance values. You can choose the color of the points by putting a value into SETCOLOR register 4, or you can use the default color, gray. The number in the COLOR statement chooses the brightness, not the color, in this mode, and your 16 paintbrushes draw with the various luminances you select. This mode is particularly interesting, because it allows you to use all 16 brightness values, not just the even-numbered ones.

Mode number 10 is perhaps the most flexible, but unfortunately it is also the most complicated. This mode allows you to use 9 different paintbrushes at once, and lets you choose their hues and luminances in any way you please. To use this effectively, however, you will need advanced programming techniques that are beyond the scope of this book. Read Bill Carris's *Inside ATARI BASIC* if you are interested.

To get a feel for what these special modes can do, type the following program:

```
10 PRINT "WHICH MODE";:INPUT MODE
20 GRAPHICS MODE
30 FOR Y=0 TO 79
40 COLOR Y
50 PLOT 0,Y
60 DRAWTO Y,Y
70 NEXT Y
80 GOTO 80
```

This is a variation on the solid-triangle program at the end of Chapter 7. The difference is that here the computer draws each horizontal line with a different color.

When you RUN the program, the computer will ask:

```
WHICH MODE?
```

You can choose any graphics mode you want, although some of the low-resolution modes will give you an error message, which you may ignore. Press BREAK to stop the program when you're finished. Then you can RUN it again choosing another mode. Mode 11 yields a beautiful 16-color rainbow pattern. Mode 9 gives five gray bars, which go through all of the gray tones from black to white (this is the pattern shown in Figure 8.5). Mode 10 gives a series of colorful bands, even though this program does not use all of its 9 colors. Modes 6, 7, 8, 14, and 15 also work with this program.

THE TEXT MODES

In addition to the 11 graphics modes, your Atari computer also has five *text modes*. You are familiar with one of them, the standard white-on-blue letters which you have been using all along. This is GRAPHICS mode 0, and it is by far the easiest to use. The others, however, do have some useful features, such as control over the color of the letters.

The other four text modes resemble the graphics modes in some ways, even though you cannot plot points or draw lines with them. When you select them with a GRAPHICS statement, the computer gives you a black graphics screen. You can display letters in different colors against this background.

You use a variation on the standard PRINT statement to display text in these special modes. Immediately after the word PRINT, type #6 and a semicolon (;). Then type your message, enclosed in quotation marks. A typical statement in one of these modes might look like this:

```
PRINT #6;"HELLO"
```

The #6 lets the computer know that you want it to display the message on the graphics screen; otherwise, it would show it as normal white letters down in the blue text window.

Large Text. Modes 1 and 2 let you display larger letters than with the normal text mode. They allow you to use only capital letters, but they let you choose the colors. These modes are therefore useful for large, important messages, and for displays where you want multiple colors. Because the letters are wider than normal text, you can only put 20 characters on each line. These two modes are identical, except that the letters in mode 2 are twice as high as in mode 1.

Figure 8.5: *The special mode number 9 offers full control over shading.*

The CAPS and inverse-video keys have a different function in these modes. If you PRINT lowercase or inverse-video messages, the results are somewhat surprising: they will come out as capital letters, but will have different colors. To see how this works, RUN the program shown in Figure 8.6, taking special care to type the lowercase and inverse-video messages as they are shown.

Figure 8.7 shows how you can use the SETCOLOR registers to change the colors of each of the four kinds of letters you may type in modes 1 and 2. Note that some of these color settings also affect the color of the text window at the bottom of the screen.

Four-color text. Modes 12 and 13 are more specialized and harder to use; however, they offer an interesting alternative. In these modes, which are available only on the new XL series, each letter is made up of dots of four different colors. By choosing your colors carefully, you can produce an interesting three-dimensional effect. Once again, the two modes are identical, except for the height of the letters.

Figure 8.6: *A program to display block letters in four colors.*

To test out this mode, change the first line of the program in Figure 8.6 to read

```
10 GRAPHICS 13
```

Then RUN the program. At first you might not even recognize the word HELLO, which the computer prints four times at the top of the screen. This is because the preset color scheme tends to fill in the middles of the letters. To make the screen more readable, type the following commands in the text window:

```
SETCOLOR 0,2,2
SETCOLOR 2,9,12
SETCOLOR 3,4,10
```

You will now be able to read the message, and see that the parts of each letter are made up of different colors.

This mode does display both uppercase and lowercase letters.

SETCOLOR REGISTER	LETTERS CONTROLLED	PRESET COLOR	SETCOLOR CODE
0	Normal capitals	Orange	0,2,8
1	Normal lowercase	Green	1,12,10
2	Inverse capitals	Blue	2,9,4
3	Inverse lowercase	Pink or Red	3,4,6
4	Background	Black	4,0,0

Figure 8.7: *How to control the colors in the text modes 1 and 2.*

SETCOLOR REGISTER	PART OF LETTER CONTROLLED	PRESET COLOR	SETCOLOR CODE
0	Left side	Orange	0,2,8
1	Middle	Green	1,12,10
2	Right side of normal letters	Blue	2,9,4
3	Right side of inverse letters	Pink or Red	3,4,6
4	Background	Black	4,0,0

Figure 8.8: *The SETCOLOR registers in the four-color text modes 12 and 13.*

Inverse video, however, controls the color scheme, as you can see from the third and fourth copies of the word HELLO on the screen. In these, the blue part of each regular letter is shifted to red, while the other colors remain the same. Figure 8.8 shows the meanings of the SETCOLOR registers in these two modes.

With the special text modes, we have reached the end of our tour of the Atari's 16 graphics modes. This has been just a brief introduction to one of the most attractive features of your computer, and I hope you will continue to explore it.

SUMMARY

The Atari computer has an attractive and flexible graphics system. Using the advanced techniques in this chapter, you can tap the potential of this system.

In graphics mode 7, the SETCOLOR command allows you to change the preset colors of your paintbrushes. You can choose any combination of 16 colors and 8 luminance values for the points and lines you draw on the screen. In the text modes, the SETCOLOR command controls the colors of the letters, background, and border.

By adding 16 to the number of any graphics mode, you can eliminate the blue text window and extend the graphic display all the way to the bottom of the screen. You can only do this in a program.

Of the 16 Atari graphics modes, 11 allow you to draw points and lines for a true graphic display. The 11 modes differ in the number of colors and the amount of resolution they offer. If you master the special GTIA modes, you can use many different colors on the screen at once to produce beautiful rainbow effects.

The other five modes are for text display. By using the large text and four-color text modes, you can display messages in oversize letters and in color.

You have now reached the end of Section Two of this book. You know how to write programs, use variables, and control the order in which the computer follows your commands. You have had a glimpse of the potential of your graphics system, and are now ready to explore your computer on your own. The fun is just beginning.

Section 3

Storage

CHAPTER NINE

Cassette Storage

In the first two sections of this book, you have been concentrating on the Atari computer itself. Everything presented up till now could be accomplished with nothing more than your computer and a television set; no additional equipment was required.

In this third section, you will learn some of the things you can do if you have additional equipment to connect to your computer. This chapter focuses on the Atari Program Recorder, which uses a cassette tape to store programs and data. Chapter 10 considers the disk drive, which has a similar function. It is more expensive, but is faster and more useful. Chapter 11 will discuss some other equipment you can add to make your system even more versatile.

There are two main reasons why you might want to add a program recorder or a disk drive to your system. First, many of the most interesting programs for the Atari are sold on cassette tape or on diskettes. If you want to use these, you will need a device that can load the program into the computer's memory.

The second reason is permanent storage. When you type a program into your computer's memory, it remains stored until you give a NEW command or turn off the power. That is fine if you just want to use the program for a few minutes, then go on to something else. Many people, however, like to write programs on their computer, then store them for future use. With a cassette recorder or disk drive, you can save the program, turn the computer off, and load the program back in when you want to use it again. In this way, you can write a complicated program and have it permanently available.

In this chapter, you will learn how to set up your Atari Program

Recorder and how to use it. You will find out how to load commerical software from cassette tapes into your computer, and how to store your own programs on tape.

SETTING UP THE PROGRAM RECORDER

There are two versions of the Atari Program Recorder. The one currently being sold is the model 1010.This compact model works well and matches the styling of the 600XL and 800XL computers.

If, however, you bought your system some time ago, you may have purchased the earlier version, model 410. This older version works exactly the same as the 1010, so you can use either model with any Atari computer.

To set up either type of program recorder, you need to make two connections. First, you must attach the thick black cable from the back of the recorder to the wide hole labeled PERIPHERAL on the back of the computer. The plug will only go into the hole one way. If it doesn't seem to fit, try turning it over. The second connection is easy: just plug the recorder into a power outlet.

The program recorder is identical to a normal cassette player, except that its special connection lets the computer turn it on and off automatically. The RECORD, PLAY, REWIND, and ADVANCE buttons work exactly as they do on a regular cassette deck, and you can use normal cassette tapes in it. Unfortunately, you cannot use a normal cassette recorder for this purpose: you must have the Atari recorder with the special cable.

If you are using prerecorded programs, you usually won't need to buy blank tapes of your own. Normally, all you'll need to do is load the program from the prerecorded cassette tape into the computer's memory.

If you want to store your own programs or want to use a special program that does expect you to store information on tape, you will need to buy some blank cassettes. You can use any normal cassette with your program recorder. Short tapes such as C-30s are usually better, since longer ones can stretch and become unreadable. You don't need to buy special high-fidelity or computer tapes. The cheapest audio tapes work just as well.

Take care of your tapes! Since your tapes may hold an expensive program or valuable data, you will want to be careful in handling them.

You must load your program from the tape every time you want to use it, and even a minor flaw can make it unreadable.

Always rewind your tapes to the beginning before you remove them from the recorder. Most tapes have a blank plastic *leader* at the start of each side, so that the recorded portion will not be exposed. If you don't rewind to this leader, you may damage the tape surface as you remove it.

Keep your tapes away from all sources of magnetism, which can erase the recorded information. Even your television and telephone can produce enough of a magnetic field to damage a recording. Keep your program recorder at least two feet away from your television, and never scatter tapes carelessly around your work area.

LOADING PRERECORDED CASSETTE PROGRAMS

Many of the programs commercially available for the Atari computers are sold on cassette tape, because cassettes are easy to use and widely available. When you buy one of these programs, you get a single cassette with the program recorded on it. To use the program, you need to load it into the computer's memory.

Since prerecorded cassette programs are made by many different companies, it is impossible to give general loading instructions that will work for all tapes. You should read the instruction sheet that comes with the package to find out the specific commands for loading that particular program.

While I cannot give you a procedure that will work for all cassette programs, I can tell you the most common one. Do the following steps in order:

1. Type:

   ```
   CLOAD
   ```

2. Press the RETURN key. You will hear one beep.
3. Put the tape in the program recorder and rewind it to the beginning of the side on which the program is stored.
4. Press PLAY on the program recorder. The tape will not start moving yet.

5. Press the RETURN key again. The tape will start to move and you will hear a beeping sound through your television.
6. Wait until the tape stops turning in the recorder. If the computer says READY, your tape has loaded correctly.
7. Press STOP on your program recorder and rewind the tape. The program is now in the computer's memory, and you can RUN it like any other program.

While the tape is loading, you cannot type other commands on the keyboard. If, at any point, you want to stop the procedure without loading the program, you can press the BREAK key. The computer will say READY, and you can type commands again.

If you get an ERROR, your computer had problems loading the tape. Rewind it and repeat this CLOAD procedure. If you still get an ERROR, you may be trying to load a tape that was designed to be loaded in some other way—check the instruction sheet that came with the program.

Unfortunately, you also might have a tape that is defective or that has become unreadable with use. Cassette tapes are very delicate, and can be easily damaged if you don't take care of them. If you cannot load a tape that you have loaded successfully in the past, it probably means that the coding has become unusable.

You can try any of three things. First, turn the tape over to the opposite side, rewind it, and repeat the procedure. Most software manufacturers duplicate the program on side two of the tape, just in case you have problems with the first copy.

If that doesn't work, you can try to RUN the program anyway, in spite of the loading error. While this rarely works, it is worth a try.

As a third and final step, check with the dealer who sold you the program. Because cassettes frequently have problems, many manufacturers will exchange a cassette that has become unreadable.

SAVING YOUR OWN PROGRAMS

If you want to store one of your own programs on a cassette, you can use a procedure called CSAVE, which is very similar to the CLOAD command. Type your program into the computer's memory.

You don't need to worry about length: you can store hundreds of program lines on even a short cassette. When you have your program the way you want it, type:

```
CSAVE
```

The computer will beep twice. This is your cue to put a cassette in the recorder, rewind it, and press the RECORD and PLAY buttons. As on a normal cassette recorder, you must press both buttons at the same time to record on the tape.

From here on, you follow exactly the same procedure as you did to load a program with CLOAD (steps 3 through 7 on pages 145–46). You press RETURN to start the tape, then wait until the recorder stops and the computer says READY. The program is now stored on the tape.

If this is a very important program, or a long one that would take hours to type back in, this tape is very valuable. Rewind it and mark it carefully. Put it in a plastic case if you have one, and store it someplace where it is safe from accidental erasure.

You can also protect your tape from accidents by punching out one of the small plastic tabs along the top of the cassette. As with an audio cassette, the Atari program recorder will not record on a tape that has this tab punched out.

To protect your cassette in this way, hold it with the recorded side facing you. Then use a pen to punch out the tab near the upper-left corner, as shown in Figure 9.1. The other tab protects the second side of the tape.

If you later decide you do want to record over a protected cassette, you can still do so. Cover up the hole with a piece of cellophane tape, then record your program, just as you normally would. The recorder will think the plastic tab has not been punched out, and will let you record over the tape. Before you press the RECORD button, make absolutely certain that this is what you want to do.

If you want to be very sure that you don't lose a program, you might want to keep it on another tape as a backup. Put a different blank cassette in the drive and type another save command. When the computer has finished saving the program you will have your backup copy on another cassette. Keep the backup in a different place. That way, if anything ever happens to your first tape, you can still load the program from the second.

You load a stored program back into the computer with a CLOAD command, just as you would a prerecorded cassette program. Follow the CLOAD procedure outlined on the previous page, then LIST the program to make sure it's the one you want.

Whenever you give a CLOAD command, the computer clears any program you may have stored in its memory, so that leftover lines won't interfere with the new program. This will erase your old program just as a NEW command would. If you have been working on an important program, you should save it before you load another in.

Since the CLOAD and CSAVE procedures are so similar, it is easy to forget which you are using. If you mistakenly press the RECORD button when you were merely trying to load a program back into the computer, you may erase a valuable program.

One way to remember is to notice the number of beeps. When the computer wants you to press only the PLAY button, it will beep once. When it wants you to press both PLAY and RECORD, it will beep twice. Just remember: one beep, one button; two beeps, two buttons.

Figure 9.1: *Protect your tapes from accidental erasure.*

It is possible to record more than one program on each side of the cassette tape, but you have to be very careful. You can keep track of several programs on a single tape by watching the small mechanical counter on top of the program recorder. If you feel certain that you won't record one on top of another, you can try to squeeze several on a side.

When you load a tape on which you want to record multiple programs, press the small reset button next to the counter on the program recorder, so that the counter reads 000. Then fast-forward the tape to well beyond the end of the first program. Note down the counter reading, then record your second program. When you want to load this second program back into the computer, you can return to its place on the tape using the counter.

Use this technique only if you're recording large numbers of programs and don't care if you lose them. You can conserve tapes by recording programs together, but you can easily erase one by accident if you're not careful. Unless you really know what you're doing, stick to one program on each side of a tape.

OTHER WAYS TO SAVE PROGRAMS

The CSAVE and CLOAD commands are the simplest way to save or load a program to or from a cassette tape. There are, however, two other pairs of commands that work in much the same way, but give slightly different results. These other commands are also more general, because they will also work for storing programs on other devices such as the disk drive.

With all of these commands, you will be using the basic seven-step procedure for controlling the program recorder. You first type your command, then press the RETURN key. The computer will beep once or twice, depending on whether it wants you to press just PLAY, or to press PLAY and RECORD together. You then set up your tape in the recorder, and press the RETURN key to set it in motion. The computer will stop the tape and say READY when it has finished saving or loading the program.

The first pair of commands is SAVE and LOAD. These do exactly the same thing as CSAVE and CLOAD, except that they are more general commands that work with other devices as well. These commands look like this:

```
SAVE "C:"
```

and

```
LOAD "C:"
```

The "C:" tells the computer that you want to use the cassette recorder to save or load the program. This letter C, which must always be followed by a colon, is the standard name for the program recorder, and you must specify it in all cassette commands except CSAVE and CLOAD.

The SAVE and CSAVE commands use different coding formats to store the program on the tape. You cannot use LOAD on a program that was saved with CSAVE, or vice versa. As with CLOAD, the LOAD command erases any program that you may have stored in the computer's memory.

Why use these expanded commands? For one thing, the SAVE format lets you load and run a cassette program in a single step:

```
RUN "C:"
```

This tells the computer to load the cassette program into its memory and RUN it immediately. With a CSAVE tape, you would have needed to give two commands:

```
CLOAD
RUN
```

LIST and ENTER are the other pair of commands. This LIST statement is a variation of the command you have used since Chapter 5 to display all or part of a program on the screen. To store program lines on a cassette with this command, type:

```
LIST "C:"
```

The "C:" tells the computer to save the program lines on the cassette tape, rather than displaying them on the screen. You can then reload them by typing:

```
ENTER "C:"
```

Once again, you can only use ENTER with a program that was saved with a LIST statement. Programs stored with CSAVE or SAVE "C:" must be loaded with their own commands.

The great advantage of LIST and ENTER is that they let you set aside parts of a program. If you only want to save the program lines from 40 through 70, you can type the command:

```
LIST "C:",40,70
```

The computer will record lines 40 and 70 and those with numbers in between. If you later use ENTER to load the program back in, these are the only lines that will be retained.

This is very useful if you want to save one useful subprogram out of an entire program. You can save the subprogram with this LIST command and later ENTER it into other programs.

Unlike CLOAD and LOAD, the ENTER command does not clear the program memory before it loads the new program. It merely adds the lines to the program that is already stored. If you do want to clear the memory, type a NEW command before you type ENTER.

You can even use this command if you need to delete a large number of lines from a program. Normally, you would have to type each of the statement numbers one by one for each of the lines that you want to delete. With a LIST "C:" command, you can save the desired part of the program on tape, clear the memory with a NEW command, and reload the part you saved with ENTER "C:".

SUMMARY

With an Atari Program Recorder, you can run commercial programs that are sold on cassette tapes, and you can save your own programs, so that you won't have to type them in each time you want to use them. This makes it practical to run much longer programs.

CSAVE and CLOAD are the two most important commands for saving and loading programs on cassette tapes. When you use these, the computer asks you to position the tape and press the appropriate buttons on the program recorder. The computer then turns the recorder on and off, as it needs to save or read information.

SAVE "C:" and LOAD "C:" are alternative commands that you can use. These are more general than CSAVE and CLOAD, since they can also be used with other devices, such as the disk drive. You can load and run programs stored in this form with a single command, RUN "C:".

You can also use LIST "C:" and ENTER "C:" to store a program. These work somewhat differently, since they let you store the program line by line. These commands are useful when you want to save only part of a program.

CHAPTER TEN

The Disk Drive

With an Atari Disk Drive, you can store your information in more useful ways than with a cassette recorder. You can use preprogrammed software almost instantly, without having to wait for the program recorder to read through the tape. A disk drive lets you save many different programs on the same diskette easily and reliably.

A disk drive is a mechanical device that can read and record information on a flat magnetic surface. It acts somewhat like a record player, spinning a circular diskette at high speed and recording information in thin bands on its surface. Unlike a phonograph record, however, the diskette can have its information changed or replaced. In this way, the disk drive acts more like a tape recorder.

A diskette, shown in Figure 10.1, is a $5^1/_4$-inch vinyl plate, covered with a magnetic recording surface. To protect it from damage, the magnetic disk is encased in a plastic envelope, with only a few small holes exposed. In operation, the drive spins the disk inside its envelope and records information on the surface as it passes.

Because they were designed specifically for computer data storage, diskettes are far superior to cassettes. Diskettes are made to spin much faster, so the computer can save or retrieve much more information in a given time. The information is recorded more efficiently on the flat surface, so a diskette can hold more than a tape.

The greatest advantage of disk storage is its flexibility. With a tape, you can only start at the beginning and read straight through to the end. With a diskette, however, your computer can go immediately to any spot you want and find the information that you want to retrieve. A diskette, therefore, lets you save many different programs, then immediately find the one you are looking for. This flexibility allows you to use disk drives to do many things that would be impractical with a program recorder.

You can connect as many as four disk drives to your Atari computer, but one is enough for most people. For most of this chapter, I assume that you have connected only one drive to your computer. Multiple drives are discussed briefly at the end.

SETTING UP THE DISK DRIVE

Atari has sold two different versions of its disk drive. The original drive was the model 810, shown at the right of Figure 10.2. The

Figure 10.1: *A typical diskette.*

newer model 1050, shown at the left of the figure, is an improved version, which works faster and can store more information on each diskette. The differences, however, are fairly minor, and both models work with all Atari computers.

Because it is a more sophisticated piece of equipment than the program recorder, the disk drive is slightly more complicated to set up. The basics are the same, however, and you can learn the rest easily.

Before you start, make sure the power switches on the computer and the disk drive are both turned off. Never connect a disk drive to the computer with the power on.

Start by connecting the large black cable from the disk drive to the the computer. This cable is just like the cord that connects the program recorder, with a wide black connector on both ends. Plug one end into one of the large I/O CONNECTOR holes on the back of the disk drive: either one will do. Then connect the other end to the hole marked PERIPHERAL on the back of the computer.

If you want to use a program recorder or another peripheral in addition to the disk drive, you can plug its cable into the other I/O CONNECTOR hole in the back of the drive. By chaining devices together in this way, you can connect as many as you want. The program recorder must always be at the end of the chain, because it does not accommodate two connectors.

Look in the small hole on the back of the disk drive marked DRIVE SELECT or DRIVE CODE. In this hole, there is a pair of

Figure 10.2: *The old and new Atari disk drives.*

small switches that tells the computer which disk drive this is. The second switch may be hard to see at first, but it is directly behind the first one and butted up against it. If you are using only one drive, both of these switches should be pushed to the left to choose drive number 1, as in Figure 10.3. To the computer, this drive will be known as D1.

The disk drive has its own power supply, which should have come packed with the unit when you bought it. Connect the small end of its cable to the PWR hole on the back of the drive, then connect the power cord to a wall outlet. That's it for the connections.

TAKING CARE OF DISKETTES

Diskettes are fragile objects. If you treat them with care, they will be reliable, but if you abuse them, you can damage them permanently.

Don't bend your diskettes. While you can flex them slightly without hurting them, you will make them unreadable if you fold them beyond their limits. Be very careful not to bend them as you handle them or insert them into the drive.

Keep dirt and dust away from your diskettes, and never touch any of the exposed portions of the recording surface. The magnetic coating on the diskette can easily be damaged by any contamination. Be

Figure 10.3: *Set both switches on your drive to the left, unless you are using more than one drive.*

especially careful of the oblong hole that extends outwards from the center. This is where the heads of the disk drive make contact with the diskette to store and retrieve information.

Always slip your diskette into its paper sleeve when you aren't using it in the machine. Store diskettes at room temperature, in a place where they won't be disturbed. Some computer stores sell plastic cases that protect diskettes in storage.

When using a diskette in a disk drive, always follow one cardinal rule: *Never insert or remove a diskette while the drive is turning.* Always wait until the drive stops and the red "busy light" goes out. Also, *remove your diskettes before you turn the drive or the computer off.* If you should neglect these rules, your disk drive might erase some of the information stored at the place where it was touching the diskette, and might even damage the recording surface.

There is one bit of protection built into the diskette system: the small *write-protect notch* along the side of the envelope. Normally, you can both read and record information on the diskette. However, if you cover up this notch, as in Figure 10.4, you protect the diskette from recording. The disk drive can still read information from the diskette, but it cannot record over or erase anything. If you later decide you do want to record on the disk, you can easily remove the covering from the notch. Most commercial programs are sold with the notches covered or absent altogether, so that you cannot erase anything. Of course, covering the notch will not protect your disks from other types of damage.

I hope you won't feel intimidated by all these "Don'ts." In my experience, diskettes are surprisingly resilient, and they will often survive abuse that you might expect would destroy them. Still, considering the amount of valuable information you may have stored, it is generally best to play it safe: if you treat your diskettes right, they will give you faithful service.

TURNING ON THE DISK DRIVE

No matter how you plan to use your disk drive, you must start it up with a prerecorded diskette. This can be either Atari's *Disk Operating System (DOS)* diskette that came with the disk drive, or a commercial software package designed directly for use on the disk drive. If this is your first time, I'd suggest you use the Atari DOS diskette.

On the front of the drive, there is a small slot or door, where you will insert your diskettes. The door looks a little different, depending on whether you have an old or a new model, but the general principle is the same.

On the model 1050, you will slide your diskettes into a very thin slot. Toward the left side, there is a small lever that you can pull down. When you do this, you are clamping the drive mechanism onto the diskette, so that it can spin and record data. When you want to remove the diskette, wait until the "busy light" goes off and then lift the lever. You can then pull the diskette out.

On the older model 810, you slide your diskette into a fairly wide slot. To lock the diskette into place, you pull the black plastic door down until it clicks. To open the door and remove the diskette, press the button just under the door, to the left of the words ATARI 810.

Whichever model you have, you use the same procedure for

Figure 10.4: *By covering the write-protect notch, you can keep the disk drive from erasing information.*

turning on the disk drive and computer. Make sure you follow this set of directions *in this order* every time you use the disk drive with your computer:

1. Before you turn the drive on, make sure that the door is open and there is no diskette inside. You can ruin a diskette if you turn the disk drive on or off with it inside. Your computer should also be off at this point.

2. Turn on the empty drive. The red PWR ON light and the "busy light" should go on and the drive should whirr into action. Don't worry if it sounds like it is trying to shred a piece of paper: that is its normal noise. After a few seconds, the "busy light" will go out and the drive will stop with a crunch. *Don't do anything until the drive stops.*

3. Once the drive is quiet and the "busy light" has gone out, insert the diskette you want to use. This must be either a prerecorded software package or the Atari DOS diskette—you cannot use a blank diskette yet. To insert the diskette, slide it into the slot on the drive with the label facing upward and the oval hole towards the back of the machine. Be extremely careful about which way you insert the diskette. Since it is square, it will fit in the slot in many ways, but it will only work when you use the proper orientation, as in Figure 10.5.

4. Push the diskette all the way into the slot, until you feel it click into place. On the 1050, there is a slight depression to the right of center in the slot, which allows you to push the disk the last eighth of an inch in. Close the door on the drive. The drive mechanism will spin for a few seconds to center the disk, then stop. It now holds the diskette mechanically, and can read information from it.

5. Turn on your computer and your television. The drive will start to whirr again, for ten to twenty seconds. While it is working, the computer shows only a blank blue screen. When the disk drive stops, the computer finally says READY, to show that you can type commands as always. You are ready to roll.

That is the ideal case. It can happen that your drive will keep turning and your computer will display the message

BOOT ERROR

This indicates that you have done something wrong as you were following this procedure. It generally means either that you were using a diskette that your computer could not read, or that you did not insert it correctly. Check yourself against Figure 10.4.

If this happens to you, the drive will just continue to whirr, and you will get a long string of BOOT ERRORs. Even though the red light does not go out, you will need to open the door on the drive to release the diskette and slide it out of the drive. Once you have done this, you can turn the power off on your computer and wait for the drive to crunch to a halt. Then turn off the disk drive and start over.

Why do you have to have a disk in the drive when you turn the computer on? When you use your Atari computer with a disk drive,

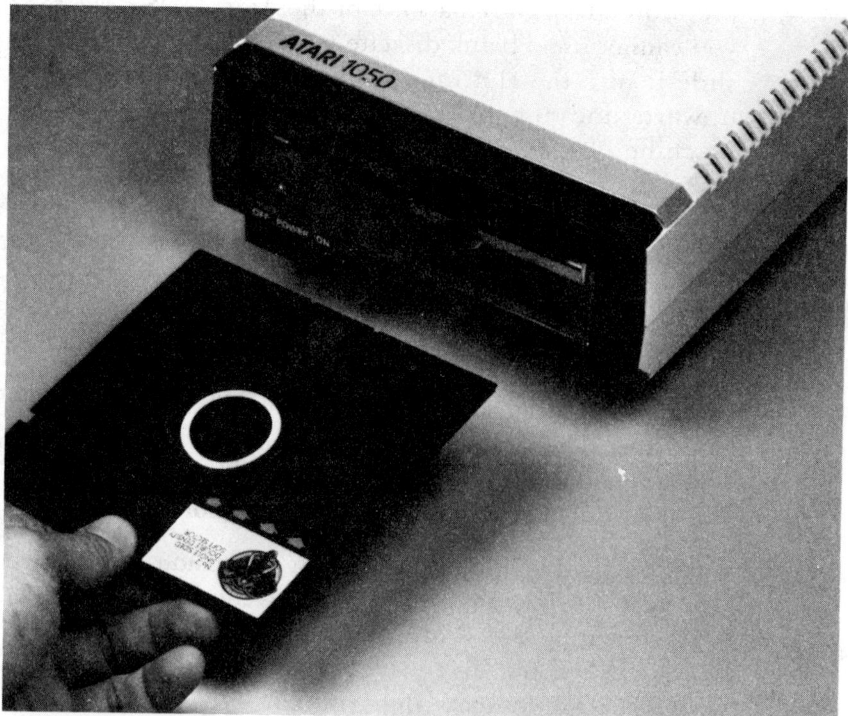

Figure 10.5: *How to insert a diskette.*

it must load some additional instructions into its memory so that it will know how to respond to disk commands. The Atari computer is designed to look for these additional instructions on the diskette you are using, then load them automatically into its memory as it is starting up. This is why you must use the Atari DOS or another prerecorded diskette: if the computer cannot find the instructions on the diskette, it will not be able to turn itself on properly.

USING PRERECORDED DISKETTE PROGRAMS

As with prerecorded cassettes, there is no way to generalize about loading commercial diskette software. The best thing you can do is read the instruction sheet that came with the program: it will surely contain detailed information on how to load the program.

Some diskette programs load and start themselves directly when you turn on the computer with the diskette in the disk drive. Others start the computer up and display the word READY. In this case, you will usually have to type a command such as

```
RUN "D:PROGRAM"
```

where PROGRAM is the name of the package you are using. Check the instruction sheet for details.

When using a commercial diskette program, you should be especially careful to follow the five-step startup procedure precisely. Diskette programs can be quite expensive, and a single mistake can make them unreadable. Most software manufacturers will replace a damaged diskette for a small fee, but they make you go through a lot of trouble to do this.

In some cases, you can make a copy of the program on a blank diskette, using the instructions on pages 168–69 later in this chapter. This allows you to use the copy and keep the original safe in case you have problems.

Many programs, however, are designed so that you cannot copy the diskette. Software companies do this to keep you from selling or giving unauthorized copies to a friend: as with books, most computer programs are copyrighted, and cannot be duplicated without permission from the author. With a program that has been protected in this way, you must be very careful not to ruin the original diskette.

THE DOS DISK

We have already encountered the Atari DOS diskette in the procedure for starting up the disk drive. This diskette, sometimes labeled MASTER DISKETTE, contains the instructions that tell the computer how to use the disk drive: if you lose this disk without making a copy, you will have no way to use the computer with the drive. DOS stands for Disk Operating System, and is actually a program that runs unseen in the computer's memory.

Atari has three different versions of its Disk Operating System: DOS 1.0, DOS 2.0S, and DOS 3.0. DOS 1.0 was the original version, and was quickly replaced by DOS 2.0S. These two versions work in almost exactly the same way, and can be used on either the old or the new disk drive.

With the introduction of the new 1050 drive, Atari has announced a new version of this DOS program. This new version, DOS 3.0, is designed to take advantage of the 1050's faster speed and higher-density storage, and it includes many other improvements over the earlier versions. It will work on the old disk drives as well.

Unfortunately, as this book is going to press, DOS 3.0 is still not available and is not expected for some time. For this reason, all of the descriptions in this book are directed toward DOS 2.0S, the most common version currently being sold. DOS 3.0 will work very similarly when it becomes available, so you will not be missing anything essential by reading about the older version.

When you turn on the computer with the DOS disk in the drive, a part of the DOS program is automatically loaded into the computer's memory. This lets the computer respond to disk commands that it would not otherwise recognize. You can use your computer just as you normally would, but you can also use these new commands that have been added to its vocabulary. These new commands include SAVE, LOAD, and RUN, which will be discussed later in this chapter.

You can also use the DOS program in a more visible way, by typing the command

```
DOS
```

This switches the computer out of its habitual mode of accepting BASIC commands and program lines, and reads in another part of the DOS program. This is a set of *disk utilities* that lets you do special operations on your diskette. Note, incidentally, that when you use the DOS command, any BASIC program you had stored will be lost. Save it first.

Type the DOS command and press RETURN. The disk drive will whirr again and the display will change to look like Figure 10.6. This is called the *DOS Menu,* because it lays out all of the selections you can make. In most cases, you will give your commands by typing one letter out of this list, then pressing RETURN. If the computer needs more information to carry out the operation, it will ask you questions on the screen.

While you still have your DOS disk in the computer, type command A; to ask for the DISK DIRECTORY. The *directory* is the list of the names of all the programs and data files stored on the disk. When you press RETURN, the computer will respond with a cryptic question:

DIRECTORY – SEARCH SPEC,LIST FILE?

It is asking you whether you want to search for a specific name or list all the files stored on the disk. Press RETURN to see the contents of

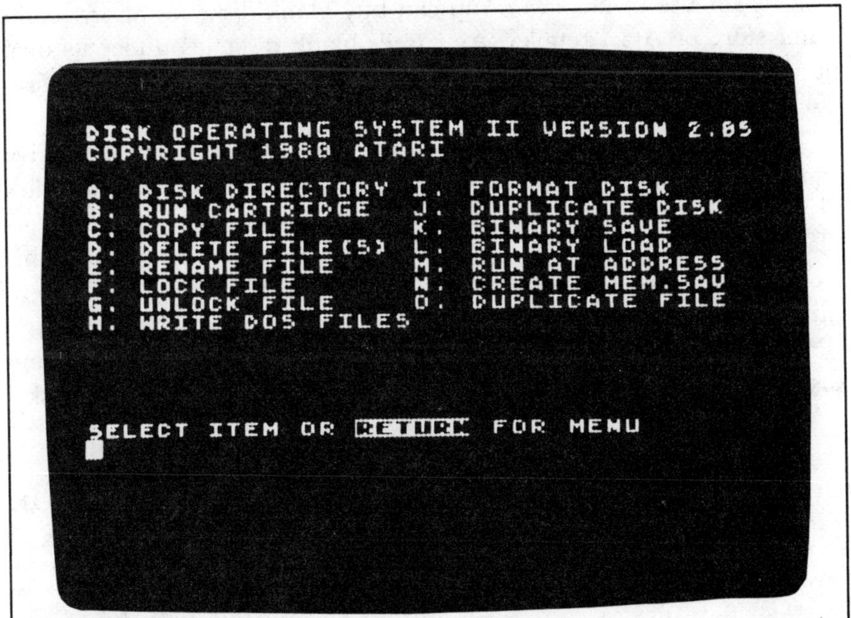

```
DISK OPERATING SYSTEM II VERSION 2.0S
COPYRIGHT 1980 ATARI

A. DISK DIRECTORY  I. FORMAT DISK
B. RUN CARTRIDGE   J. DUPLICATE DISK
C. COPY FILE       K. BINARY SAVE
D. DELETE FILE(S)  L. BINARY LOAD
E. RENAME FILE     M. RUN AT ADDRESS
F. LOCK FILE       N. CREATE MEM.SAV
G. UNLOCK FILE     O. DUPLICATE FILE
H. WRITE DOS FILES

SELECT ITEM OR RETURN FOR MENU
```

Figure 10.6: The DOS Menu.

the entire disk. If you have version 2.0S of the DOS program, the computer will probably list three names, something like this:

```
    DOS       SYS 039
    DUP       SYS 042
    AUTORUN   SYS 001
625 FREE SECTORS
```

The names of the programs and the number of FREE SECTORS may vary slightly with your diskette. This number shows how much space you have left on the diskette (625 is a lot).

When you have many other files stored on the disk, the directory might fill up the entire screen and even roll some of the names off the top. To keep this from happening, you can stop the movement of the list by pressing CONTROL and the number 1. Proceed like this: give the directory command as usual, then press CONTROL-1 as the listing appears on the screen. It will stop where it is, so that you can read it. When you're ready to go on, press CONTROL-1 again and the listing will continue to the end.

Since you have only one DOS diskette, it is best to prepare a blank diskette for use in its place. You can buy blank diskettes at any computer store or Atari retailer. Atari sells blank diskettes under its own name, but you can also use any number of other good brands. Diskettes are usually sold in cartons of five or ten.

To use a blank diskette, you must first *format* it so that the disk drive can read it. When you ask the computer to do this, it tells the disk drive to put magnetic markings on the diskette so that it can find its place as it moves around. You don't have to worry about how this works: just format the disk, and the computer will keep track of where things are.

Remove the DOS diskette from the drive and insert your blank diskette. Then type I, for FORMAT DISK. The computer will ask

```
WHICH DRIVE TO FORMAT?
```

Unless you have more than one drive, you should answer 1 or D1. The computer will then ask you to

```
TYPE "Y" TO FORMAT DISK 1
```

It asks you this to make sure you really want to go ahead with it. Make sure your diskette is actually blank: Formatting will erase any information that you had stored on the disk. If you're certain this is all right, type Y and press RETURN. The drive will click for about 45 seconds, then stop. You cannot give further commands until the "busy light" has gone out.

Before you can use your blank diskette as a duplicate DOS disk, you need to do one more thing. Type the H command, WRITE DOS FILES. This tells the computer to take the DOS program stored in its memory and copy it onto your blank diskette. Answer D1 and Y to the same two questions, then wait while the computer shows the message

```
WRITING NEW DOS FILES
```

When the drive stops, your blank diskette contains all of the information the computer needs to control the drive. You can use this disk as if it were the original DOS disk.

I would suggest you go through this procedure every time you begin using a new diskette. Fire up the disk drive using a diskette that already contains the DOS program (this can be either the original disk or another disk you have already prepared). Format the new blank diskette and write the DOS files to it. You can then use this disk as a "parent" for others, and keep the original DOS diskette safe.

FILES

The rest of the blank diskette is yours to play with. You can store programs, data, or other information in any way you wish.

Your computer organizes the disk in *files.* These are logical blocks of information that you want to use all at once in the computer. A stored program is normally a single file—you save it as a unit, then reload it all at once. Other common files include blocks of data (such as a mailing list), and *system utilities,* such as the DOS program.

Every file has its own name. The computer automatically keeps track of the place where each file is recorded, so all you need to do is refer to it by its name. The disk directory (selection A on the DOS menu) is an index of the names of all the files on the diskette. You can store up to 64 files on an Atari diskette.

The name of a file can be up to eight letters long. The file name can contain numbers, though not as the first character. Spaces and punctuation marks are not allowed. As with variables, it is best to choose a name that explains the file's contents. Otherwise, you are likely to forget where the information is stored.

You can add an optional three-letter *extension* following the file name. Many people use this to explain what type of information is stored (BAS means a BASIC program, DAT means a data file, SYS stands for a system program, such as DOS). You can also use the extension to distinguish different versions of a program.

The full name of a file consists of three parts: the drive number (D1, unless you're using more than one drive), the file name, and the extension. Always type a colon (:) between the drive number and the file name, and a period (.) between the file name and the extension. You can usually leave off the drive number if you are just using a single drive, and you can omit the extension if it is blank. The following are some valid file names, in their full forms:

```
D1:DOS.SYS
D1:FILENAME.EXT
D1:PROG137.BAS
D1:NAMEONLY (no extension)
```

Now that you know how to give names to files, you can use some of the other options on the DOS menu. With options C, D, and E, you can copy, delete, or rename any file on the disk. As an example, let's make a copy of the DOS.SYS file, and call it NEWCOPY. Type C and press RETURN. The computer should respond

```
COPY–FROM, TO?
```

It is asking you to tell which file you want to copy, and what name you want to give to the new file. Type this line exactly:

```
DOS.SYS,NEWCOPY
```

Note that we omitted the drive number D1 from the file names (the computer assumes this unless you tell it otherwise). The two file names are separated by a comma in this line.

When you press RETURN, the disk drive will start to whirr, making a second copy of all the information stored in the DOS.SYS file. When it has finished, you can check to see that the copy is also on the disk, by asking for a disk directory (command A). If you are working with a newly-formatted diskette, the computer will respond something like this:

```
    DOS       SYS 039
    DUP       SYS 042
    NEWCOPY       039
587 FREE SECTORS
```

Try out the E-RENAME and D-DELETE commands on this NEWCOPY file. They both work in similar ways to the C-COPY command, though with DELETE the computer stops to ask you

```
TYPE "Y" TO DELETE . . .
D1:NEWCOPY. ?
```

It does this to make sure you really do want to delete the file. Once you type Y and press RETURN, the file is gone forever.

SAVING YOUR OWN PROGRAMS

If you have been writing your own programs, you can store them conveniently as files on a diskette. You can save many different programs on a single diskette, then call them back by name as you need them. You can build a library of all the programs you have written, so that you never have to retype an old program. You simply find the file on the diskette and run the stored program.

To type and save a program, you must leave the DOS menu and return to the normal BASIC programming language. You do this by typing the B command, shown on the DOS menu as RUN CARTRIDGE. If you have one of the new XL machines with built-in BASIC, you might find this phrase confusing: it is left over from the time when Atari BASIC was a cartridge that had to be plugged in. With the new XL machines, this command simply sends the computer back to its familiar READY prompt, to show that you can again type normal commands and program lines. Atari will probably change the words RUN CARTRIDGE in a future revision of its DOS program.

When you have the word READY on the screen, type in your program, exactly the way you want it. RUN it to make sure it works, then use the following command to store it on the diskette:

```
SAVE "D:FILENAME.EXT"
```

FILENAME and EXT can be any name and extension that you want to give to your stored program. You must always precede the file name with D: (or D1: if you need to specify the drive number), and put the whole thing in quotation marks. If you forget the D:, the computer will have no way to know that you want it to use the disk drive rather than some other device, such as the program recorder.

When you store a program on a diskette, you must always give it a name, so that the computer can locate it when you want to retrieve it. This was not necessary with the program recorder, since the computer always loaded the first program it found on the tape.

If you SAVE a program with the same name as a file already on the diskette, it will erase the existing file to write the new one. This is helpful if you have made a minor change in a program you have stored and want to replace the old version: just save the corrected program on top of it. Of course, you must also be careful that you don't erase an existing program by mistake: give your programs names that are distinctive enough that you will never repeat them accidentally.

When you later want to retrieve the program, type

```
LOAD "D:FILENAME.EXT"
```

The computer will find the file with the name you specify, then load it into the memory. You can LIST or RUN this program, as if you had just typed it in. As with cassettes, you can LOAD and RUN a program in one step, with the command

```
RUN "D:FILENAME.EXT"
```

The SAVE, LOAD, and RUN commands for diskette storage are the same as the cassette commands SAVE "C:", LOAD "C:", and RUN "C:", which were covered at the end of Chapter 9. The C: and D: within the quotation marks tell the computer whether to use the cassette recorder or the disk drive; otherwise the statements are identical. There are also LIST and ENTER commands for diskettes—read pages 150–51 of Chapter 9 to find out how these work. There are no disk commands that correspond to CSAVE and CLOAD.

DUPLICATING DISKS

There is another useful command on the DOS menu that makes a backup copy of an entire disk: J for DUPLICATE DISK.

If you don't already have the DOS menu on your screen, type DOS. Then type J and press RETURN. The computer will respond

```
DUP DISK – SOURCE,DEST DRIVES?
```

This line is asking you which drive you want to copy the information *from* and which drive you want to copy it *to*. If, like most people, you have only one drive, your answer will be 1 or D1 to both questions. Type the following and press RETURN:

```
D1,D1
```

With only one disk drive, you must swap the original and duplicate disks in and out of your drive. The computer will use its memory as a storage buffer. It first reads the information in from the original disk, then stops to let you remove the original and insert the copy disk. Then, it writes a copy on this second disk of the information it had just read. If, as usually happens, it could not hold all of the original disk's stored information at one time, the computer then asks you to reinsert the original and then again the copy so that it can duplicate more of the information. It will keep asking you to swap your diskettes until it has transferred all of the original's information.

When you have finally finished with the disk-swapping, the "destination disk" contains an exact copy of all of the files stored on the original diskette. You should use this DUPLICATE DISK feature frequently to make backup copies of your important diskettes. That way, if anything should happen to the diskette you are using, you will not lose your work. You can use the duplicate copy in place of the original, and continue with your work.

If you have more than one disk drive, you can avoid much of this disk-swapping. You simply put the original disk in one of your drives and the duplicate disk in the other. The computer will transfer all of the information directly from one disk to the other without having to ask you to change disks.

This convenience is one of the primary reasons why some people choose to add a second drive to their system. While it doesn't allow you to do anything you can't do with a single drive, a second drive does simplify many disk-management operations.

You set up the second drive just like the first, except that you plug its cable into the back of the first drive, rather than into the PERIPHERAL hole on the computer. Use a pen to move the black switch inside the hole on the back of the second drive.

You can use this second drive just like the first one; simply refer to it by the name D2. You can SAVE, LOAD, and RUN programs on this drive by using D2 as part of the file name:

```
SAVE "D2:FILENAME.EXT"
```

The only thing you cannot do with the second drive is start the system up: the computer always looks for its DOS instructions on drive number 1.

SUMMARY

For permanent storage, a disk drive is faster, more flexible, and more reliable than a program recorder. You can record many different programs on a single diskette, and retrieve them by name. You can also load commercial disk programs and run them in a matter of seconds.

Some commercial programs will load themselves directly without any special command. With others, you may need to give a LOAD or a RUN command.

To save or load your own programs, you will need to use Atari's Disk Operating System (DOS) disk. When you turn on your computer with this disk in the drive, the computer will automatically load some extra commands to let you SAVE and LOAD programs directly. You can also type the DOS command to do more specialized disk operations, such as formatting a blank diskette, deleting files, or duplicating an entire diskette.

CHAPTER ELEVEN

Afterword

In the course of this book, you have seen many of the things you can do with your Atari computer. You have learned how to set it up and how to use preprogrammed software. You have learned to give commands of your own and to write programs that will control the computer in various ways. Finally, in this third section, you have found out about Atari's Program Recorder and Disk Drive, which you can connect to your system to store programs permanently.

This is only the beginning. With these basic skills, you can go on to explore many other possibilities. You can connect a printer or other equipment to your system, and write complex programs that solve important problems.

In these final pages, I will try to give you an idea of some of these other possibilities. I cannot cover everything, though. If you want more detailed information, check some of the books in the bibliography, or try some experiments on your own.

OTHER ADD-ONS

Atari's three *printers* were briefly mentioned at the end of Chapter 1. They differ in many ways, but all three have the same function: they take the information that is stored electronically in the computer and display it on paper.

A printer is useful for many reasons. You might want to make a permanent listing of a program, so that you are sure you can type it back in if you should lose it. If you are writing a long program, the printer will let you read it all at once, rather than one screen at a time. And of course, you will need a printer if you want to use your computer as a word processor.

You connect an Atari printer to the computer using the hole labeled PERIPHERAL, just as you would connect a program recorder or disk drive. If you want to use several peripherals at once, you can connect them all in a chain, as described in the chapter on the disk drive (see page 155).

With the printer connected and turned on, you can normally use it without further trouble. Many financial and word-processing programs will let you print tables and text directly, with a simple command.

If you have a program of your own stored in your computer's memory, you can print a copy of it out on paper. To do this, use the following variation on the standard LIST command:

```
LIST "P:"
```

The computer will then type the program out, line by line, just as it would have displayed it on your television screen. The "P:" in the statement tells the computer to send the program listing to the printer rather than to the screen.

You can use the printer to do many things other than simply listing programs on paper. You can display messages or lists of numbers on paper, rather than on the screen. On the 1025 printer, you can ask the printer to type in special ways or to change the spacing between letters. With the 1020 printer/plotter, you can even draw certain types of graphics.

Another useful accessory is a *telephone modem.* This is a device that lets you connect your computer to a telephone line so that it can communicate electronically with another computer. With this, you can send a program to a friend across the country, or receive information from one of the new electronic news and information services, such as The Source.

If all goes as planned, Atari's 1030 *direct-connect modem* will let you do this very easily. This device converts your computer's electronic signals into a warbling sound, which it then sends directly over your telephone lines. The modem has a small hole where you can plug in a standard telephone cable. With the help of a special program, your computer can send information directly to another computer. It can also receive messages from another computer and store them in its memory.

Atari is planning a large line of other add-on devices to match its new XL series of computers. Some of these may never materialize, but they are worth looking out for.

One interesting product is the *Touch Tablet*, a special electronic pad which lets you draw graphic designs directly, without any programming. You draw with a special pen on the tablet, and the computer can sense exactly where you move. It can then paint with an imaginary paintbrush on the screen, precisely following your movements on the pad.

An even more interesting idea is the *light pen*, which Atari has been developing for several years. This is an electronic rod that you can point at your television screen. With a special circuit, your computer can sense exactly which spot you are pointing to, and can move a cursor to that point or paint it a certain color. As you do this, it will seem as if your light pen were actually painting lines on your television screen.

Atari has also planned an *Expansion System*, a large box that will allow you to connect many different expansions to your computer, including devices not made by Atari.

At this writing, all of these add-ons are speculation. They have all been officially announced by Atari, but some may never be sold. Check with your dealer for more information and for detailed descriptions.

OTHER DIRECTIONS

If you have been reading the programming sections of this book, you have learned some of the ways you can control your computer directly. You can create a program, use variables to perform calculations, and control the program's flow with loops and decisions. With special graphics commands, you can paint pictures in various ways on the screen.

While you have now covered all the fundamental concepts, there are many other thing you can do. We have really only scratched the surface.

Within the BASIC programming language, there are specialized features that let you control your computer in other ways. You can, for example, use *arrays* that let you store an entire table of numbers in the memory, rather than giving them each separate variable names. You can save words or numbers as *data* on cassette or diskette. You can then later retrieve this information and reuse it in other programs.

There are several other programming languages that you can use with your Atari computer. One of the most popular is Atari PILOT, a graphics language for children. In this language, you give commands to move a small *turtle* around the screen. As it moves, the turtle lays down a trail, which your child can use to create interesting pictures.

With any programming language, the computer must translate the English-like commands into the specific codes that it can use. This process is slow and inefficient, so some people bypass the process completely for complex programs that must run quickly. They do this with *machine language,* which allows direct control of the computer.

With machine language, you are actually giving commands at the deepest level of the computer, and can exert direct control over its operation. Some of the advanced graphics features of the Atari computer can only be controlled with direct machine language commands: the animated figures and missiles of video games are an example of this. Machine language also lets the computer run much more quickly, since inefficient operations are reduced.

Unfortunately, machine language is very technical and difficult to use, since it forces you to keep track of every single operation the computer must do. You must know a lot about the internal workings of the machine, and must be willing to do tedious programming. Even professional programmers usually avoid machine language unless there is a clear need for it.

Machine language is closely related to *assembly language,* which is slightly more understandable. While you must still give meticulous commands for every operation you want the computer to do, you can use labels and verbal commands, rather than numerical codes. The computer can translate assembly language directly into machine language when it uses it.

Some books and magazines take a middle ground between BASIC and machine language, by using two special BASIC statements: PEEK and POKE. These let you read and store values directly in the computer's memory, without giving them a variable name. In this way, you can exert some types of direct control over the internal operation of the computer, which you could not do otherwise without machine language. The process is, however, quite cumbersome and hard to understand.

Whatever you do, I hope that you will continue your explorations beyond the end of this book. There are many other books and resources that can help you learn even more than I have been able to cover in these pages. Your main resource, however, is yourself. Be creative with your computer, and play around with it. There are many wonderful things you can do with your machine, with whatever approach you choose to take.

APPENDIX A

Further Reading

There are many different books about the Atari computers, and I can hardly list all of them. These are just a few of the most useful places to look for more information.

Inside ATARI BASIC

by Bill Carris (Reston, 1983).

This is one of the most appealing introductions to BASIC programming on the Atari computers, complete with attractive illustrations and useful programming tips. This book is particularly strong on graphics, since it covers the GTIA modes clearly and in depth. Very entertaining reading.

Atari Sound and Graphics

by Herb Moore, Judy Lower, and Bob Albrecht (Wiley, 1982).

This is a readable introduction to BASIC, with special attention paid to the Atari sound and graphics systems. While its treatment is not as thorough as it could be, it is an interesting approach to learning the machine.

Your First Atari Program

by Rodnay Zaks (Sybex, 1984).

A fine introduction to fundamental techniques of BASIC programming, which concentrates on the ways you should think as you try to write a program. The delightful illustrations by Daniel Le Noury help to make things clear.

Your Atari Computer

by Lon Poole, Martin McNiff, and Steven Cook (Osborne/McGraw-Hill, 1982).

This 450-page book gives every piece of information that you would ever want to know about the Atari computer and peripherals. This is required reading for anyone serious about programming the Atari computer, and an essential reference book. It is not, however, light reading. The descriptions are fairly technical, and assume some previous knowledge of computers. Also, until a revised edition becomes available, this book does not cover the enhancements incorporated in the XL series.

Atari BASIC Programs in Minutes

by Stanley R. Trost (Sybex, 1984).

This is a collection of short programs which you can type directly into your Atari computer and use, with no prior knowledge of BASIC programming. The programs cover a range of financial, home management, and educational applications.

The Book of Atari Software 1983

edited by Jeffrey Stanton, Robert P. Wells, and Sandra Rochowansky (Addison-Wesley, 1983).

A catalog of all of the programs available for the Atari computers, as of early 1983. Each program is given a quick letter-grade rating, and a brief review. While a half-page review will not tell you everything you need to know before you buy a program, it will give you some idea of what is available. Revised versions will presumably become available.

APPENDIX B

Reference Guide to BASIC

This is not a complete reference list of the BASIC language, but a summary of the commands described in this book. For a complete reference guide, read Chapter 11 of *Your Atari Computer,* by Poole, McNiff, and Cook (Osborne/McGraw-Hill, 1982).

CLOAD

Asks the computer to load a program into its memory from a cassette tape. The computer will beep once to ask you to press PLAY on the program recorder, then will load the program. Any program already in the memory will be erased.

COLOR n

Chooses the graphic paintbrush which will be used to draw in future PLOT and DRAWTO statements. The computer will continue to use that paintbrush until you give another COLOR command. In specialized graphics modes, the COLOR command may have other meanings (see Chapter 8).

CSAVE

Asks the computer to save the program by storing it on a cassette tape. The computer will beep twice to ask you to press PLAY and RECORD on the program recorder, and will record the program. The program also remains in the computer's memory.

DATA

Used with the READ statement to assign numbers to variables. The numbers in the list after the word DATA are assigned in sequence to the corresponding variables in the READ statement. If not all the numbers in the DATA statement have been assigned yet, further READ statements will continue to use them, starting at the number where the last READ statement left off.

DIM

Sets aside space for a string variable or an array of numbers.

```
DIM A$(12)
```

would set aside space for 12 letters in the string variable A$.

DOS

Tells the computer to run the Disk Operating System program, so that you can perform certain disk operations, such as formatting a blank diskette, copying a file, or duplicating an entire diskette. You can use this command only if you have turned your computer on with the Atari DOS disk in the drive, following the procedure in Chapter 10.

DRAWTO *x,y*

In the graphics modes, this draws a line to the coordinates *x,y* from the current location of the paintbrush. The paintbrush will be the one chosen in the most recent COLOR statement. The coordinates must be within the allowable range for the graphics mode you are using.

END

Marks the last statement in a program. You can omit this statement if your program proceeds normally from start to finish. If, however, you have a subprogram or other statement that follows the end of the main program, you must use this command to stop the computer.

ENTER

Used with the program recorder or disk drive to reload a program that was stored using the LIST command. For a cassette, type

```
ENTER "C:"
```

For a disk drive, you must give the name of the file you want to retrieve:

```
ENTER "D:FILENAME.EXT"
```

The ENTER command does not clear the computer's program memory, but adds the lines to the program already stored.

FOR/NEXT

The FOR statement marks the beginning of a loop, and tells the computer how many times to repeat the loop. The general form is:

FOR *I*=*a* TO *b* STEP *c*

You must specify a counter variable (*I*), its starting value (*a*), and its ending value (*b*). You can also name the step (*c*) that you want the counter to take each time through the loop. If you omit the STEP, the computer assumes it is 1. FOR must always be paired with a NEXT statement, which marks the end of the loop.

GOSUB n

Asks the computer to run the subprogram that starts at statement number *n*. The computer will run the subprogram until it reaches the RETURN statement that marks its end. The computer then resumes the main program with the statement following the GOSUB.

GOTO n

Tells the computer to jump directly to statement number *n* and continue from there.

GRAPHICS n

Clears the screen and shifts to a new graphics mode. The number *n* names the new mode: the most common values are 0 (text), 7 (four-color graphics), and 8 (high-resolution graphics). If you shift into the mode that you are already using, the mode will not change, but the graphics screen will be cleared. By adding 16 to the graphics mode number, you can eliminate the text window at the bottom of the screen.

IF/THEN

Tells the computer to make a decision. If the condition following the word IF is met, the computer carries out the command that follows the word THEN. If the condition is not met, the computer skips the command and goes directly to the next statement.

INPUT

Has the computer stop each time it runs the program and ask you to type in a number or letters to assign to a variable. It displays a question mark, then waits for you to type your answer and press RETURN. It then stores your number in the variable named in the INPUT statement.

LIST

Used by itself, the word LIST has the computer display the stored program on the screen. If you follow LIST with a statement number, the computer will display only that particular statement. If you follow LIST with two numbers, the computer will display those two statements and all those in between.

LIST can also be used to store a program on tape or diskette.

```
LIST "C:"
```

asks the computer to send the program listing directly to the program recorder, rather than to the screen. With a disk drive, you must type a file name:

```
LIST "D:FILENAME.EXT"
```

A program saved with LIST can only be reloaded using the ENTER command.

LOAD

Retrieves a program that has been stored on a cassette tape or diskette. To load from a cassette, type:

```
LOAD "C:"
```

With a diskette, a file name is required:

```
LOAD "D:FILENAME.EXT"
```

The computer will erase any program in its memory before it loads the new one. LOAD will only work with files that were stored with a SAVE command.

NEW

Clears the computer's program memory so that you can type a new program. If you forget to use this command, lines from your old program may be mixed in with your new statements.

NEXT

Marks the end of a FOR/NEXT loop. This statement must always be paired with a preceding FOR statement. The variable name after the word NEXT must exactly match the name of the counter variable in the FOR statement.

PLOT x,y

In the graphics modes, this command paints a single point at the coordinates *x,y*. If the paintbrush was in a different part of the screen, it is moved to the new point without drawing a line. The next line drawn will proceed from the new point. The coordinates must be within the range allowed for the graphics mode you are using.

POSITION x,y

In the text mode, POSITION moves the cursor to the coordinates *x,y*. The next PRINT statement will then display its message starting at that point.

PRINT

Displays a message on the screen. If you enclose a word in quotation marks, the computer prints it as you typed it. If you do not use quotation marks, the computer treats the word as a variable name and displays its current value. You can include several messages in a single PRINT statement, using a semicolon (;) to separate them. A semicolon at the end of the statement keeps the computer from dropping down to the next line before displaying the next message.

With the special text modes 1, 2, 12, and 13, you display messages on the graphics screen with the command

```
PRINT #6;"message"
```

READ

Works with the DATA statement to assign a list of numbers to a series of variables. Each variable name in the READ statement is assigned the corresponding number in the DATA statement. The first READ statement in a program loads its numbers starting with the first DATA statement; additional READ statements continue with the first unused number in the DATA statement's list.

RETURN

Marks the end of a subprogram. When the computer reaches this statement, it resumes the main program with the statement following the GOSUB that had called the subprogram.

RUN

Asks the computer to execute the program stored in its memory. Program lines are used in order of their statement numbers, unless a GOTO, GOSUB, or FOR/NEXT statement alters the flow. At the end, the computer stops and says READY. The program remains stored in the memory.

SAVE

Records the program stored in the computer's memory onto a cassette tape or diskette. With a cassette, you merely type:

```
SAVE "C:"
```

With a disk drive, you must specify the file name under which the computer will store the program:

```
SAVE "D.FILENAME.EXT"
```

You must use LOAD to reload a program stored with the SAVE command.

SETCOLOR

Assigns a new color to one of the graphic paintbrushes, according to the codes shown in Figure 8.1, on page 125. In the text and high-resolution graphics modes, SETCOLOR controls the color of entire regions of the screen (background, border, and letters).

=

The equals sign acts as a command, to assign a value to a variable. The computer first carries out any calculations involved in the expression to the right of the equals sign, then stores the result in the variable to the left. For example, the statement

```
J=2+2
```

would assign the value 4 to the variable J.

APPENDIX C

Atari Error Codes

This is a list of the most common Atari error codes, along with their meanings and most likely causes. Not all of the codes are listed here, though these should cover most of what you encounter as you use this book. When using graphics or a disk drive, in particular, you may occasionally get a more obscure error. You can find a complete list in the *Atari BASIC Reference Guide,* which came with your machine. For a better explanation of unusual error codes, check the appendix of *Your Atari Computer,* by Poole, McNiff, and Cook (Osborne/McGraw-Hill, 1982).

2 Memory Insufficient

Your computer's memory is limited to 16K or 64K bytes, depending on which Atari model you own. Program lines, variables, and graphic displays all use up memory. On the Atari 600XL, this error is quite common in the higher-resolution graphics modes.

3 Value Error

You have used a number that is too large or too small for the command. This is a very common error, which can occur if you use a statement number that is too large (the limit is 32767), or if you try to PLOT or DRAWTO coordinates which are outside the limits of the graphics mode you are using. Many other statements can give a value error as well.

4 Too Many Variables

You are limited to 128 variables in any program. Even when you use and later delete a reference to a variable, it may still be counted toward that limit. A NEW command clears the entire list of variables.

6 Out of Data Error

There were not enough values in the program's DATA statements to fill all of the variables in a READ statement.

7 Number Greater than 32767

Statement numbers and certain other values must be less than 32767.

8 INPUT Statement Error

The number or string that you typed in response to an INPUT question could not be stored in the variable. This often happens when you type a letter or a punctuation mark in the middle of a number. It can also happen when you press RETURN without giving a response.

9 Array or String Dimension Error

Before you can use a string or an array, you must set aside space for it, using a DIM statement.

11 Floating Point Overflow/Underflow Error

The computer can calculate very large numbers (up to 10^{98}), but it is still possible to exceed this. You may have tried to divide by zero, for example.

12 Line Not Found

You tried to jump to a nonexistent statement number. Check your GOTO or GOSUB statement.

13 No Matching FOR Statement

A NEXT statement must always be paired with a FOR statement containing the same counter variable. You may have forgotten a FOR or NEXT statement, or written a loop not completely contained within another loop.

14 *Line Too Long Error*

Commands are limited to 114 characters or 3 screen lines.

15 *GOSUB or FOR Line Deleted*

A RETURN or NEXT statement is not matched properly with a GOSUB or FOR statement.

16 *RETURN Error*

The computer encountered a RETURN statement without having been sent to a subprogram. There may be a missing GOSUB statement, or you may have forgotten to type END as the last line of your main program.

19 *LOAD Program Too Long*

You tried to load a program from a disk or tape, and the program would not fit into the computer's memory.

21 *LOAD File Error*

A LOAD command will only retrieve a program that was recorded with a SAVE command. Programs stored with CSAVE or LIST must be reloaded with CLOAD and ENTER, respectively.

130 *Unknown Device*

You tried to use a peripheral device that was not connected to the system, or you may have forgotten to precede a diskette file name with D:, the device name.

133 *Device or File not Open*

Can occur if you try to use a PLOT or DRAWTO command in a text mode. Also, after a graphics program has ended, the graphics screen must be cleared and reopened with a GRAPHICS statement, before PLOT or DRAWTO can be used.

138 Device Timeout

The computer did not get a response from a peripheral device that you asked it to use. Your peripheral may not be connected properly.

141 Cursor Out of Range

You tried to POSITION the cursor at a point that was outside the limits of the text mode you are using.

144 Device Done Error

You tried to save a program on a diskette whose write-protect notch was covered.

147 Insufficient Screen RAM

You tried to use a graphics mode that exceeded the limits of your computer's memory. High-resolution graphics on the Atari 600XL often give this error.

162 Disk Full

The space on the diskette is large, but limited. If you are storing a number of very long programs on the same disk, you may get this error.

165 File Name Error

Diskette file names must start with a letter and may contain only capital letters and numbers.

169 Directory Full

A diskette is limited to 64 files, even when there is still space to store more information. Try deleting some unneeded files.

170 File Not Found

You tried to load or use a file that is not on your diskette. You may have misspelled the name, or you may be using the wrong diskette.

Answers to Selected Exercises

3.2: Give the command:

```
PRINT "ONE":PRINT "TWO":PRINT "THREE"
```

To do the same kind of thing in a single command, type the following line, using ESC, CONTROL, and the down arrow key every place you see the ↓ symbol:

```
PRINT "ONE↓TWO↓THREE"
```

3.3: The computer starts to print the message on the line immediately below the command. Before it has a chance to start the word UPPER, though, the first up arrow moves the cursor back over P in PRINT. The computer then prints the word UPPER on top of the word PRINT, moves two lines further up, and prints the word LOWER. It then reaches the end of the message, so it drops down two lines and says READY, just as it always does. Once again, however, the word lands right on top of another word—the UPPER that was just printed. The final result will look like this:

```
            LOWER

READY "↑ UPPER ↑↑ LOWER"
```

4.1: You can choose many possible positions for the three names. This might be one:

```
POSITION 10,7:PRINT "TOM":POSITION 27,
11:PRINT "TOM":POSITION 0,20:PRINT "TO
M"
```

4.2: Type the seven commands shown on pages 57–58. Then add six more, such as this:

```
COLOR 3
PLOT 20,20
DRAWTO 60,20
DRAWTO 60,60
DRAWTO 20,60
DRAWTO 20,20
```

5.1: Add this line to the program:

```
65  COLOR 3
```

5.2: Add this line:

```
80  DRAWTO 70,70
```

If you have just done exercise 1, the diagonal line will be blue.

5.3: The three bugs are:

1. The word PRINT is misspelled in line 10.
2. The second coordinate (734) in line 40 is outside the allowed range.
3. The DRAWTO statement in line 60 has only one coordinate.

6.1: Add a statement number 15, and replace statement 20, as follows:

```
15  PRINT "COLOR NUMBER";:INPUT N
20  COLOR N
```

6.2: Add these statements to the program on page 96:

```
120  REM INVERTED TRIANGLE
130  PLOT X,Y+20
140  DRAWTO X+20,Y-10
150  DRAWTO X+40,Y+20
160  DRAWTO X,Y+20
```

6.3: It will set the new value of J to equal the old value (10) plus 1, or 11.

7.1:

```
10  PRINT "WHAT NUMBER";:INPUT NUMBER
20  IF NUMBER>0 THEN PRINT "POSITIVE"
30  IF NUMBER<0 THEN PRINT "NEGATIVE"
40  IF NUMBER=0 THEN PRINT "ZERO"
```

7.2:

```
1000  REM SUBPROGRAM TO CLEAR SCREEN
1010  PRINT "{ESC-CONTROL-CLEAR}"
1020  RETURN
```

7.3: Try this program:

```
10  SUM=0
20  FOR I=1 TO 100
30  SUM=SUM+I
40  NEXT I
50  PRINT SUM
```

The answer should be 5050.

INDEX

Selections from The SYBEX Library

Buyer's Guides

THE BEST OF TI 99/4A™ CARTRIDGES

by Thomas Blackadar

150 pp., illustr., Ref. 0-137

Save yourself time and frustration when buying TI 99/4A software. This buyer's guide gives an overview of the best available programs, with information on how to set up the computer to run them.

FAMILY COMPUTERS UNDER $200

by Doug Mosher

160 pp., illustr., Ref. 0-149

Find out what these inexpensive machines can do for you and your family. "If you're just getting started . . . this is the book to read before you buy."—Richard O'Reilly, Los Angeles newspaper columnist

PORTABLE COMPUTERS

by Sheldon Crop and Doug Mosher

128 pp., illustr., Ref. 0-144

"This book provides a clear and concise introduction to the expanding new world of personal computers."—Mark Powelson, Editor, *San Francisco Focus Magazine*

THE BEST OF VIC-20™ SOFTWARE

by Thomas Blackadar

150 pp., illustr., Ref. 0-139

Save yourself time and frustration with this buyer's guide to VIC-20 software. Find the best game, music, education, and home management programs on the market today.

SELECTING THE RIGHT DATA BASE SOFTWARE

SELECTING THE RIGHT WORD PROCESSING SOFTWARE

SELECTING THE RIGHT SPREADSHEET SOFTWARE

by Kathy McHugh and Veronica Corchado

80 pp., illustr., Ref. 0-174, 0-177, 0-178

This series on selecting the right business software offers the busy professional concise, informative reviews of the best available software packages.

Introduction to Computers

OVERCOMING COMPUTER FEAR

by Jeff Berner

112 pp., illustr., Ref. 0-145

This easy-going introduction to computers helps you separate the facts from the myths.

COMPUTER ABC'S

by Daniel Le Noury and Rodnay Zaks

64 pp., illustr., Ref. 0-167

This beautifully illustrated, colorful book for parents and children takes you alphabetically through the world of computers, explaining each concept in simple language.

PARENTS, KIDS, AND COMPUTERS

by Lynne Alper and Meg Holmberg

208 pp., illustr., Ref. 0-151

This book answers your questions about the educational possibilities of home computers.

THE COLLEGE STUDENT'S COMPUTER HANDBOOK

by Bryan Pfaffenberger

350 pp., illustr., Ref. 0-170

This friendly guide will aid students in selecting a computer system for college study, managing information in a college course, and writing research papers.

COMPUTER CRAZY

by Daniel Le Noury

100 pp., illustr., Ref. 0-173

No matter how you feel about computers, these cartoons will have you laughing about them.

DON'T! (or How to Care for Your Computer)

by Rodnay Zaks

214pp., 100 illustr., Ref. 0-065

The correct way to handle and care for all elements of a computer system, including what to do when something doesn't work.

YOUR FIRST COMPUTER

by Rodnay Zaks

258 pp., 150 illustr., Ref. 0-045

The most popular introduction to small computers and their peripherals: what they do and how to buy one.

INTERNATIONAL MICROCOMPUTER DICTIONARY

120 pp., Ref. 0-067

All the definitions and acronyms of microcomputer jargon defined in a handy pocket-sized edition. Includes translations of the most popular terms into ten languages.

FROM CHIPS TO SYSTEMS: AN INTRODUCTION TO MICROPROCESSORS

by Rodnay Zaks

552 pp., 400 illustr., Ref. 0-063

A simple and comprehensive introduction to microprocessors from both a hardware and software standpoint: what they are, how they operate, how to assemble them into a complete system.

Personal Computers

ATARI

YOUR FIRST ATARI® PROGRAM

by Rodnay Zaks

150 pp., illustr., Ref. 0-130

A fully illustrated, easy-to-use introduction to ATARI BASIC programming. Will have the reader programming in a matter of hours.

BASIC EXERCISES FOR THE ATARI®

by J.P. Lamoitier

251 pp., illustr., Ref. 0-101

Teaches ATARI BASIC through actual practice using graduated exercises drawn from everyday applications.

ATARI® BASIC PROGRAMS IN MINUTES

by Stanley R. Trost

170 pp., illustr., Ref. 0-143

You can use this practical set of programs without any prior knowledge of BASIC! Application examples are taken from a wide variety of fields, including business, home management, and real estate.

Commodore 64/VIC-20

THE COMMODORE 64™/VIC-20™ BASIC HANDBOOK

by Douglas Hergert

144 pp., illustr., Ref. 0-116

A complete listing with descriptions and instructive examples of each of the Commodore 64 BASIC keywords and functions. A handy reference guide, organized like a dictionary.

THE EASY GUIDE TO YOUR COMMODORE 64™

by Joseph Kascmer

160 pp., illustr., Ref. 0-129

A friendly introduction to using the Commodore 64.

YOUR FIRST VIC-20™ PROGRAM

by Rodnay Zaks

150 pp., illustr., Ref. 0-129

A fully illustrated, easy-to-use introduction to VIC-20 BASIC programming. Will have the reader programming in a matter of hours.

THE VIC-20™ CONNECTION

by James W. Coffron

260 pp., 120 illustr., Ref. 0-128

Teaches elementary interfacing and BASIC programming of the VIC-20 for connection to external devices and household appliances.

YOUR FIRST COMMODORE 64™ PROGRAM

by Rodnay Zaks

182 pp., illustr., Ref. 0-172

You can learn to write simple programs without any prior knowledge of mathematics or computers! Guided by colorful illustrations and step-by-step instructions, you'll be constructing programs within an hour or two.

COMMODORE 64™ BASIC PROGRAMS IN MINUTES

by Stanley R. Trost

170 pp., illustr., Ref. 0-154

Here is a practical set of programs for business, finance, real estate, data analysis, record keeping and educational applications.

GRAPHICS GUIDE TO THE COMMODORE 64™

by Charles Platt

192 pp., illustr., Ref. 0-138

This easy-to-understand book will appeal to anyone who wants to master the Commodore 64's powerful graphics features.

IBM

THE ABC'S OF THE IBM® PC

by Joan Lasselle and Carol Ramsay

100 pp., illustr., Ref. 0-102

This is the book that will take you through the first crucial steps in learning to use the IBM PC.

THE BEST OF IBM® PC SOFTWARE

by Stanley R. Trost

144 pp., illustr., Ref. 0-104

Separates the wheat from the chaff in the world of IBM PC software. Tells you what to expect from the best available IBM PC programs.

THE IBM® PC-DOS HANDBOOK

by Richard Allen King

144 pp., illustr., Ref. 0-103

Explains the PC disk operating system, giving the user better control over the system. Get the most out of your PC by adapting its capabilities to your specific needs.

BUSINESS GRAPHICS FOR THE IBM® PC

by Nelson Ford

200 pp., illustr., Ref. 0-124

Ready-to-run programs for creating line graphs, complex illustrative multiple bar graphs, picture graphs, and more. An ideal way to use your PC's business capabilities!

THE IBM® PC CONNECTION
by James W. Coffron
200 pp., illustr., Ref. 0-127
Teaches elementary interfacing and BASIC programming of the IBM PC for connection to external devices and household appliances.

BASIC EXERCISES FOR THE IBM® PERSONAL COMPUTER
by J.P. Lamoitier
252 pp., 90 illustr., Ref. 0-088
Teaches IBM BASIC through actual practice, using graduated exercises drawn from everyday applications.

USEFUL BASIC PROGRAMS FOR THE IBM® PC
by Stanley R. Trost
144 pp., Ref. 0-111
This collection of programs takes full advantage of the interactive capabilities of your IBM Personal Computer. Financial calculations, investment analysis, record keeping, and math practice—made easier on your IBM PC.

YOUR FIRST IBM® PC PROGRAM
by Rodnay Zaks
182 pp., illustr., Ref. 0-171
This well-illustrated book makes programming easy for children and adults.

YOUR IBM® PC JUNIOR
by Douglas Hergert
250 pp., illustr., Ref. 0-179
This comprehensive reference guide to IBM's most economical microcomputer offers many practical applications and all the helpful information you'll need to get started with your IBM PC Junior.

DATA FILE PROGRAMMING ON YOUR IBM® PC
by Alan Simpson
275 pp., illustr., Ref. 0-146
This book provides instructions and examples of managing data files in BASIC. Programming designs and developments are extensively discussed.

Apple

THE EASY GUIDE TO YOUR APPLE II®
by Joseph Kascmer
160 pp., illustr., Ref. 0-122
A friendly introduction to using the Apple II, II plus and the new IIe.

BASIC EXERCISES FOR THE APPLE®
by J.P. Lamoitier
250 pp., 90 illustr., Ref. 0-084
Teaches Apple BASIC through actual practice, using graduated exercises drawn from everyday applications.

APPLE II® BASIC HANDBOOK
by Douglas Hergert
144 pp., illustr., Ref. 0-155
A complete listing with descriptions and instructive examples of each of the Apple II BASIC keywords and functions. A handy reference guide, organized like a dictionary.

APPLE II® BASIC PROGRAMS IN MINUTES
by Stanley R. Trost
150 pp., illustr., Ref. 0-121
A collection of ready-to-run programs for financial calculations, investment analysis, record keeping, and many more home and office applications. These programs can be entered on your Apple II plus or IIe in minutes!

YOUR FIRST APPLE II® PROGRAM
by Rodnay Zaks
150 pp., illustr., Ref. 0-136
A fully illustrated, easy-to-use introduction to APPLE BASIC programming. Will have the reader programming in a matter of hours.

THE APPLE® CONNECTION
by James W. Coffron
264 pp., 120 illustr., Ref. 0-085
Teaches elementary interfacing and BASIC programming of the Apple for connection to external devices and household appliances.

TRS-80

YOUR COLOR COMPUTER

by Doug Mosher

350 pp., illustr., Ref. 0-097

Patience and humor guide the reader through purchasing, setting up, programming, and using the Radio Shack TRS-80/TDP Series 100 Color Computer. A complete introduction.

THE FOOLPROOF GUIDE TO SCRIPSIT™ WORD PROCESSING

by Jeff Berner

225 pp., illustr., Ref. 0-098

Everything you need to know about SCRIPSIT—from starting out, to mastering document editing. This user-friendly guide is written in plain English, with a touch of wit.

Timex/Sinclair 1000/ZX81

YOUR TIMEX/SINCLAIR 1000 AND ZX81™

by Douglas Hergert

159 pp., illustr., Ref. 0-099

This book explains the set-up, operation, and capabilities of the Timex/Sinclair 1000 and ZX81. Includes how to interface peripheral devices, and introduces BASIC programming.

THE TIMEX/SINCLAIR 1000™ BASIC HANDBOOK

by Douglas Hergert

170 pp., illustr., Ref. 0-113

A complete alphabetical listing with explanations and examples of each word in the T/S 1000 BASIC vocabulary; will allow you quick, error-free programming of your T/S 1000.

TIMEX/SINCLAIR 1000™ BASIC PROGRAMS IN MINUTES

by Stanley R. Trost

150 pp., illustr., Ref. 0-119

A collection of ready-to-run programs for financial calculations, investment analysis, record keeping, and many more home and office applications. These programs can be entered on your T/S 1000 in minutes!

MORE USES FOR YOUR TIMEX/SINCLAIR 1000™
Astronomy on Your Computer

by Eric Burgess

176 pp., illustr., Ref. 0-112

Ready-to-run programs that turn your TV into a planetarium.

Other Popular Computers

YOUR FIRST TI 99/4A™ PROGRAM

by Rodnay Zaks

182 pp., illustr., Ref. 0-157

Colorfully illustrated, this book concentrates on the essentials of programming in a clear, entertaining fashion.

THE RADIO SHACK® NOTEBOOK COMPUTER

by Orson Kellogg

128 pp., illustr., Ref. 0-150

Whether you already have the Radio Shack Model 100 notebook computer, or are interested in buying one, this book will clearly explain what it can do for you.

THE EASY GUIDE TO YOUR COLECO ADAM™

by Thomas Blackadar

175 pp., illustr., Ref. 0-181

This quick reference guide shows you how to get started on your Coleco Adam with a minimum of technical jargon.

YOUR KAYPRO II/4/10™

by Andrea Reid and Gary Deidrichs

250 pp., illustr., Ref. 0-166

This book is a non-technical introduction to the KAYPRO family of computers. You will find all you need to know about operating your KAYPRO within this one complete guide.

Languages

C

UNDERSTANDING C
by Bruce Hunter
200 pp., Ref 0-123
Explains how to use the powerful C language for a variety of applications. Some programming experience assumed.

FIFTY C PROGRAMS
by Bruce Hunter
200 pp., illustr., Ref. 0-155
Beginning as well as intermediate C programmers will find this a useful guide to programming techniques and specific applications.

BUSINESS PROGRAMS IN C
by Leon Wortman and Thomas O. Sidebottom
200 pp., illustr., Ref. 0-153
This book provides source code listings of C programs for the business person or experienced programmer. Each easy-to-follow tutorial applies directly to a business situation.

BASIC

YOUR FIRST BASIC PROGRAM
by Rodnay Zaks
150pp. illustr. in color, Ref. 0-129
A "how-to-program" book for the first time computer user, aged 8 to 88.

FIFTY BASIC EXERCISES
by J. P. Lamoitier
232 pp., 90 illustr., Ref. 0-056
Teaches BASIC by actual practice, using graduated exercises drawn from everyday applications. All programs written in Microsoft BASIC.

INSIDE BASIC GAMES
by Richard Mateosian
348 pp., 120 illustr., Ref. 0-055
Teaches interactive BASIC programming through games. Games are written in Microsoft BASIC and can run on the TRS-80, Apple II and PET/CBM.

BASIC FOR BUSINESS
by Douglas Hergert
224 pp., 15 illustr., Ref. 0-080
A logically organized, no-nonsense introduction to BASIC programming for business applications. Includes many fully-explained accounting programs, and shows you how to write them.

PASCAL PROGRAMS FOR SCIENTISTS AND ENGINEERS
by Alan R. Miller
374 pp., 120 illustr., Ref. 0-058
A comprehensive collection of frequently used algorithms for scientific and technical applications, programmed in Pascal. Includes such programs as curve-fitting, integrals and statistical techniques.

DOING BUSINESS WITH PASCAL
by Richard Hergert and Douglas Hergert
371 pp., illustr., Ref. 0-091
Practical tips for using Pascal in business programming. Includes design considerations, language extensions, and applications examples.

Assembly Language Programming

PROGRAMMING THE 6502
by Rodnay Zaks
386 pp., 160 illustr., Ref. 0-046
Assembly language programming for the 6502, from basic concepts to advanced data structures.

6502 APPLICATIONS
by Rodnay Zaks
278 pp., 200 illustr., Ref. 0-015
Real-life application techniques: the input/output book for the 6502.

ADVANCED 6502 PROGRAMMING

by Rodnay Zaks

292 pp., 140 illustr., Ref. 0-089

Third in the 6502 series. Teaches more advanced programming techniques, using games as a framework for learning.

PROGRAMMING THE Z80

by Rodnay Zaks

624 pp., 200 illustr., Ref. 0-069

A complete course in programming the Z80 microprocessor and a thorough introduction to assembly language.

Z80 APPLICATIONS

by James W. Coffron

288 pp., illustr., Ref. 0-094

Covers techniques and applications for using peripheral devices with a Z80 based system.

PROGRAMMING THE 6809

by Rodnay Zaks and William Labiak

362 pp., 150 illustr., Ref. 0-078

This book explains how to program the 6809 in assembly language. No prior programming knowledge required.

PROGRAMMING THE Z8000

by Richard Mateosian

298 pp., 124 illustr., Ref. 0-032

How to program the Z8000 16-bit microprocessor. Includes a description of the architecture and function of the Z8000 and its family of support chips.

PROGRAMMING THE 8086/8088

by James W. Coffron

300 pp., illustr., Ref. 0-120

This book explains how to program the 8086 and 8088 in assembly language. No prior programming knowledge required.

EXECUTIVE PLANNING WITH BASIC

by X. T. Bui

196 pp., 19 illustr., Ref. 0-083

An important collection of business management decision models in BASIC, including Inventory Management (EOQ), Critical Path Analysis and PERT, Financial Ratio Analysis, Portfolio Management, and much more.

BASIC PROGRAMS FOR SCIENTISTS AND ENGINEERS

by Alan R. Miller

318 pp., 120 illustr., Ref. 0-073

This book from the "Programs for Scientists and Engineers" series provides a library of problem-solving programs while developing proficiency in BASIC.

CELESTIAL BASIC

by Eric Burgess

300 pp., 65 illustr., Ref. 0-087

A collection of BASIC programs that rapidly complete the chores of typical astronomical computations. It's like having a planetarium in your own home! Displays apparent movement of stars, planets and meteor showers.

YOUR SECOND BASIC PROGRAM

by Gary Lippman

250 pp., illustr., Ref. 0-152

A sequel to *Your First BASIC Program*, this book follows the same patient, detailed approach and brings you to the next level of programming skill.

Pascal

INTRODUCTION TO PASCAL (Including UCSD Pascal™)

by Rodnay Zaks

420 pp., 130 illustr., Ref. 0-066

A step-by-step introduction for anyone wanting to learn the Pascal language. Describes UCSD and Standard Pascals. No technical background is assumed.

THE PASCAL HANDBOOK

by Jacques Tiberghien

486 pp., 270 illustr., Ref. 0-053

A dictionary of the Pascal language, defining every reserved word, operator, procedure and function found in all major versions of Pascal.

APPLE® PASCAL GAMES

by Douglas Hergert and Joseph T. Kalash

372 pp., 40 illustr., Ref. 0-074

A collection of the most popular computer games in Pascal, challenging the reader not only to play but to investigate how games are implemented on the computer.

INTRODUCTION TO THE UCSD p-SYSTEM™

by Charles W. Grant and Jon Butah

300 pp., 10 illustr., Ref. 0-061

A simple, clear introduction to the UCSD Pascal Operating System; for beginners through experienced programmers.

Software and Applications

Operating Systems

THE CP/M® HANDBOOK

by Rodnay Zaks

320 pp., 100 illustr., Ref 0-048

An indispensable reference and guide to CP/M—the most widely-used operating system for small computers.

MASTERING CP/M®

by Alan R. Miller

398 pp., illustr., Ref. 0-068

For advanced CP/M users or systems programmers who want maximum use of the CP/M operating system . . . takes up where our *CP/M Handbook* leaves off.

THE BEST OF CP/M® SOFTWARE

by John D. Halamka

250 pp., illustr., Ref. 0-100

This book reviews tried-and-tested, commercially available software for your CP/M system.

REAL WORLD UNIX™

by John D. Halamka

250 pp., illustr., Ref. 0-093

This book is written for the beginning and intermediate UNIX user in a practical, straightforward manner, with specific instructions given for many special applications.

THE CP/M PLUS™ HANDBOOK

by Alan R. Miller

250 pp., illustr., Ref. 0-158

This guide is easy for the beginner to understand, yet contains valuable information for advanced users of CP/M Plus (Version 3).

Business Software

INTRODUCTION TO WORDSTAR™

by Arthur Naiman

202 pp., 30 illustr., Ref. 0-077

Makes it easy to learn how to use WordStar, a powerful word processing program for personal computers.

PRACTICAL WORDSTAR™ USES

by Julie Anne Arca

200 pp., illustr., Ref. 0-107

Pick your most time-consuming office tasks and this book will show you how to streamline them with WordStar.

MASTERING VISICALC®

by Douglas Hergert

217 pp., 140 illustr., Ref. 0-090

Explains how to use the VisiCalc "electronic spreadsheet" functions and provides examples of each. Makes using this powerful program simple.

DOING BUSINESS WITH VISICALC®

by Stanley R. Trost

260 pp., Ref. 0-086

Presents accounting and management planning applications—from financial statements to master budgets; from pricing models to investment strategies.

DOING BUSINESS WITH SUPERCALC™

by Stanley R. Trost

248 pp., illustr., Ref. 0-095

Presents accounting and management planning applications—from financial statements to master budgets; from pricing models to investment strategies.

VISICALC® FOR SCIENCE AND ENGINEERING

by Stanley R. Trost and Charles Pomernacki

225 pp., illustr., Ref. 0-096

More than 50 programs for solving technical problems in the science and engineering fields. Applications range from math and statistics to electrical and electronic engineering.

DOING BUSINESS WITH 1-2-3™

by Stanley R. Trost

250 pp., illustr., Ref. 0-159

If you are a business professional using the 1-2-3 software package, you will find the spreadsheet and graphics models provided in this book easy to use "as is" in everyday business situations.

THE ABC'S OF 1-2-3™

by Chris Gilbert

225 pp., illustr., Ref. 0-168

For those new to the LOTUS 1-2-3 program, this book offers step-by-step instructions in mastering its spreadsheet, data base, and graphing capabilities.

UNDERSTANDING dBASE II™

by Alan Simpson

220 pp., illustr., Ref. 0-147

Learn programming techniques for mailing label systems, bookkeeping and data base management, as well as ways to interface dBASE II with other software systems.

DOING BUSINESS WITH dBASE II™

by Stanley R. Trost

250 pp., illustr., Ref. 0-160

Learn to use dBASE II for accounts receivable, recording business income and expenses, keeping personal records and mailing lists, and much more.

DOING BUSINESS WITH MULTIPLAN™

by Richard Allen King and Stanley R. Trost

250 pp., illustr., Ref. 0-148

This book will show you how using Multiplan can be nearly as easy as learning to use a pocket calculator. It presents a collection of templates that can be applied "as is" to business situations.

DOING BUSINESS WITH PFS®

by Stanley R. Trost

250 pp., illustr., Ref. 0-161

This practical guide describes specific business and personal applications in detail. Learn to use PFS for accounting, data analysis, mailing lists and more.

INFOPOWER: PRACTICAL INFOSTAR™ USES

by Jule Anne Arca and Charles F. Pirro

275 pp., illustr., Ref. 0-108

This book gives you an overview of InfoStar, including DataStar and ReportStar, WordStar, MailMerge, and SuperSort. Hands on exercises take you step-by-step through real life business applications.

WRITING WITH EASYWRITER II™

by Douglas W. Topham

250 pp., illustr., Ref. 0-141

Friendly style, handy illustrations, and numerous sample exercises make it easy to learn the EasyWriter II word processing system.

Business Applications

INTRODUCTION TO WORD PROCESSING

by Hal Glatzer

205 pp., 140 illustr., Ref. 0-076

Explains in plain language what a word processor can do, how it improves productivity, how to use a word processor and how to buy one wisely.

COMPUTER POWER FOR YOUR LAW OFFICE

by Daniel Remer

225 pp., Ref. 0-109

How to use computers to reach peak productivity in your law office, simply and inexpensively.

OFFICE EFFICIENCY WITH PERSONAL COMPUTERS

by Sheldon Crop

175 pp., illustr., Ref. 0-165

Planning for computerization of your office? This book provides a simplified discussion of the challenges involved for everyone from business owner to clerical worker.

COMPUTER POWER FOR YOUR ACCOUNTING OFFICE

by James Morgan

250 pp., illustr., Ref. 0-164

This book is a convenient source of information about computerizing you accounting office, with an emphasis on hardware and software options.

Other Languages

FORTRAN PROGRAMS FOR SCIENTISTS AND ENGINEERS

by Alan R. Miller

280 pp., 120 illustr., Ref. 0-082

In the "Programs for Scientists and Engineers" series, this book provides specific scientific and engineering application programs written in FORTRAN.

A MICROPROGRAMMED APL IMPLEMENTATION

by Rodnay Zaks

350 pp., Ref. 0-005

An expert-level text presenting the complete conceptual analysis and design of an APL interpreter, and actual listing of the microcode.

Hardware and Peripherals

MICROPROCESSOR INTERFACING TECHNIQUES

by Rodnay Zaks and Austin Lesea

456 pp., 400 illustr., Ref. 0-029

Complete hardware and software interconnect techniques, including D to A conversion, peripherals, standard buses and troubleshooting.

THE RS-232 SOLUTION

by Joe Campbell

225 pp., illustr., Ref. 0-140

Finally, a book that will show you how to correctly interface your computer to any RS-232-C peripheral.

USING CASSETTE RECORDERS WITH COMPUTERS

by James Richard Cook

175 pp., illustr., Ref. 0-169

Whatever your computer or application, you will find this book helpful in explaining details of cassette care and maintenance.

For a complete catalog of our publications please contact:

U.S.A.
SYBEX, Inc.
2344 Sixth Street
Berkeley,
California 94710
Tel: (800) 227-2346
(415) 848-8233
Telex: 336311

FRANCE
SYBEX
6–8 Impasse du Curé
75018 Paris
France
Tel: 01/203–9595
Telex: 211801

GERMANY
SYBEX-Verlag GmbH
Vogelsanger Weg 111
4000 Düsseldorf 30
West Germany
Tel: (0211) 626411
Telex: 8588163

YOUR FIRST **ATARI** PROGRAM

Written especially for the ATARI computer, this is a how-to-program book for the first-time computer user. It is filled with colorful illustrations and simple diagrams that make learning easy. In just a few hours, you'll know enough BASIC to write complete, useful programs on your ATARI. See how simple it is to program your computer to do what you want it to!

BASIC EXERCISES FOR THE **ATARI**

Learn the true style and subleties of ATARI BASIC through actual practice. Graduated exercises in math, business, operations, research, games, and statistics teach you how to program in BASIC. Each exercise contains a statement and analysis of the problem, a solution with flowchart, and a program with a detailed explanation of each step. Appendices of BASIC terms, syntax rules, and character sets make this a handy reference guide.